NFL
Ultimate Beginners Guide

A Basic Guide to Learn and Enjoy the Game

EDWARD

WEBER

Copyright

NFL Ultimate Beginners Guide

Copyright © 2023 Edward Weber

All rights reserved. No part of this publication may be reproduced or transmitted in any form or by any means, electronic, or mechanical, including photocopying, recording, or by any information storage and retrieval system, without permission in writing from the publisher.

While the advice and information in this book are believed to be true and accurate at the date of publication, neither the authors nor the editors nor the publisher can accept any legal responsibility for any errors or omissions that may be made. The publisher makes no warranty, express or implied, with respect to the material contained herein.

Disclaimer

This book is geared towards providing information in regards to the topic and issue covered. The publication is sold with the idea that the publisher is not required to render accounting, officially permitted, or otherwise, qualified services. If advice is necessary. Legal or health professional, a practiced individual in the profession should be ordered.

Printed on acid-free paper.

Contents

Copyright i
Background 1
History and Evolution 1
Why American Football? 7
CHAPTER ONE 9
TERMINOLOGIES OF AMERICAN FOOTBALL 9
Official Terms 9
Slangs and Nitty-gritty 28
CHAPTER TWO 32
THE BASICS 32
Equipment 32
Order of Play 37
Field Dimensions 38
Downs and Yards to Go 41
CHAPTER THREE 49
PLAYERS, POSITIONS AND ROLES 49
Uniform Numbers and Positions 49
Players and Roles 50
Offensive Positions 51
Defensive Positions 59
Special Team 65
CHAPTER FOUR 68
RULES OF AMERICAN FOOTBALL 68

Timekeeping 68
Overtime Rule 69
Play Clock 72
Kickoff Rules 73
Freekick Rules 76
Scoring Rules 80
Penalties 83
Additional Rules 96

CHAPTER FIVE 105
NFL SEASON SCHEDULING 105
NFL Divisions 105
Post-Season 108
The Vince Lombardi Trophy 111
Records 113
Free Agency 114
NFL Draft 115
Revenue 118

CHAPTER SIX 119
TACTICS, STRATEGY AND SKILLS 119
Offensive Football Strategy 119
Defensive Football Strategy 131
Special Team Strategies 140
Game Management Strategies 141

iii

Football Skills 143
Techniques in Football 155
Key Plays 167
About the Author 170

Background

American football is a physically demanding sport that calls for a variety of skills, including quickness, agility, speed, and both physical and mental tenacity. The sport is a spectacle because of the massive collisions and complex plays involving the 22 men on the field. Games can last up to three hours and appear fairly complex, in large part because each play is frequently very tactical. Football is actually a fairly simple sport to follow and take pleasure in. The complexity of the sport, developed through years of devoted observation, is what makes it so captivating to watch and distinguishes it from other contests of strength and muscle.

In order to distinguish it from football (or soccer, as it is commonly known), it is also referred to as American football. American football is frequently referred to as gridiron or gridiron football in several countries to distinguish it from other football sports. At the amateur level, the sport is well-liked in nations like Mexico and, to a lesser extent, in regions of Europe, New Zealand, Japan, and Australia. Even though men dominate the sport, a few amateur and semi-pro women's leagues have emerged in recent years.

History and Evolution

In the modern era, American football is loved by all. Before big games, people are eager to check out NFL choices, and they are eager to watch the matches live at the stadium or from the convenience of their homes. However, those outside of the United States are perplexed as to why this sport is referred to as football, given that it is more comparable to rugby. We therefore need to look into the history of American football's beginnings in order to get the answer to that question. With that in mind, here's a quick look at the history of American football.

American football has its roots in early versions of soccer and rugby. In 1869, two college teams participated in the first ever official game of American football, which was more similar to football (soccer) than rugby. Over time, the rules of the game began to resemble those of rugby, as they were developed during the 1876 college football season, but the name of the sport was not changed to rugby. Instead of just calling it football, English-speaking nations outside of America adopted terminology like "American football" and "gridiron."

As previously stated, American football evolved from soccer to rugby-style regulations that allowed the ball to be picked up and carried across the field. American football was a cruel and deadly sport in its early years, frequently causing numerous injuries and sometimes deaths. After a record-breaking 19 deaths nationally, President Theodore Roosevelt threatened to outlaw the sport if adjustments weren't made. The National Collegiate Athletic Association (NCAA) was then established after 62 institutions convened in New York in 1905 to consider alterations to the game's rules.

Who Invented it?

While many people have contributed to the growth of the sport, Walter Camp is often regarded as the "Father of American Football." He created a set of guidelines for the game in 1880, making it more orderly and secure. These rules covered downs, the line of scrimmage, and the neutral zone. Camp also favored using eleven players on both teams and a smaller field of play. His recommendations significantly influenced how American football is played now. The Walter Camp Award is given each year in his honor to the best college football player.

How did this all start?

The mythology claims that William Webb Ellis, a student, was the first to pick up the ball and run with it during a school football game in 1823. As a result, he invented a new form of play in which picking up the ball and running with it was preferred to kicking it. From this point on, American colleges and universities would start playing their own kind of football.

However, Rutgers and Princeton, two American universities, competed in the first ever recognized American football game in 1869. The regulations of the game, which were significantly different from modern football and more akin to a rugby match, were also quite simple at the time. The rules didn't start to resemble the game that we know today until the late 1800s.

There were 25 players on each of the squads. Players could only take one kick per possession, and there was no forward pass allowed. The only way to move the ball around the field was to kick it or bat it with hands, knees, or heads. For the game, ten points were the maximum that could be earned. Rutgers won the contest 6-4, and the game laid the groundwork for one of the most adored sports in history.

Creation of NFL
Just a few years after the first official American football game, the American Professional Football Association, today known as the National Football League (NFL), was established in Ohio in 1920. It wasn't yet the major league that exists today and consisted primarily of clubs from small midwestern locations at the time. However, the association's use of timetables and appropriate payment methods contributed significantly to the professionalization of the sport.

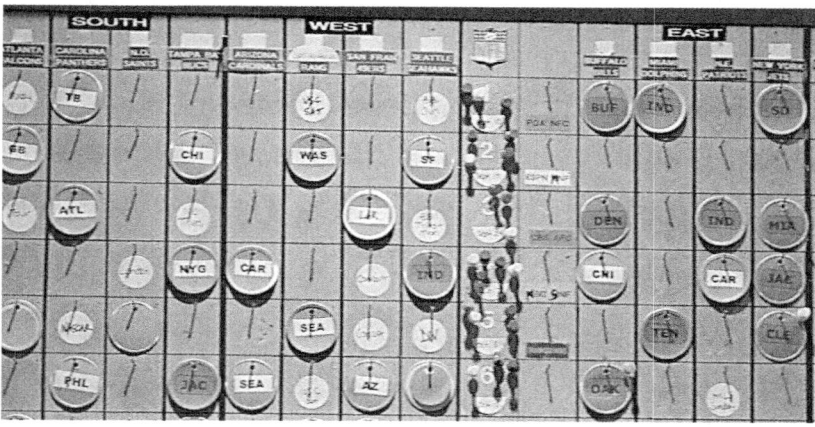

With all of the modifications and new regulations, the APFA pushed football closer to the form it is in today.

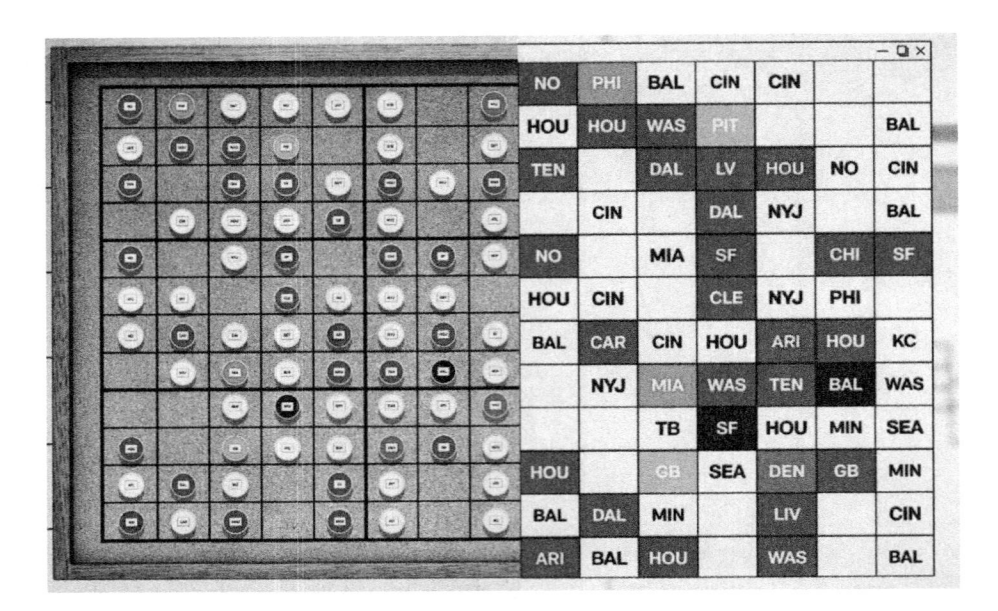

The American Professional Football Association (APFA) modified its name to the National Football League (NFL) in 1922, and numerous additional clubs joined the league in the years that followed. Today, the NFL is the largest football league in the United States, with 32 teams divided evenly between the National Football Conference (NFC) and the American Football Conference (AFC).

What does the future hold?

American football has advanced significantly since its humble beginnings in 1869. What began as a simple match played between two universities has developed into one of the world's most well-liked sports with a long history and heritage. The game is adored by millions of people worldwide and has generated some of the biggest names in the world.

Looking ahead, we may anticipate that football, like every other industry, will be impacted by technology. Future football is anticipated to be significantly influenced by technology, with the league utilizing new developments to boost fan involvement and produce an interactive experience. The Turf Tank, a robotic football field painter that automates the line-marking procedure, is one of the most recent developments in football. The robot is a more effective procedure than the manual one since it cuts down on the amount of time needed to mark football fields and reduces paint use by half.

Why American Football?

American football is more than just getting the ball into the opposing team's end zone. It's a very tactical sport that also involves a lot of strategy. Although athletic prowess is important, it is not sufficient to win the match. Around the world, people enjoy watching this sport because, typically, the teams are trying to outsmart one another and rack up as many points as they can. Because of this, American football is so well-liked, and sporting occasions like the Super Bowl are viewed and advertised all around the world.

Despite having little in common with football (soccer), American football still goes by that name, and its iconic fame is well-known all over the world.

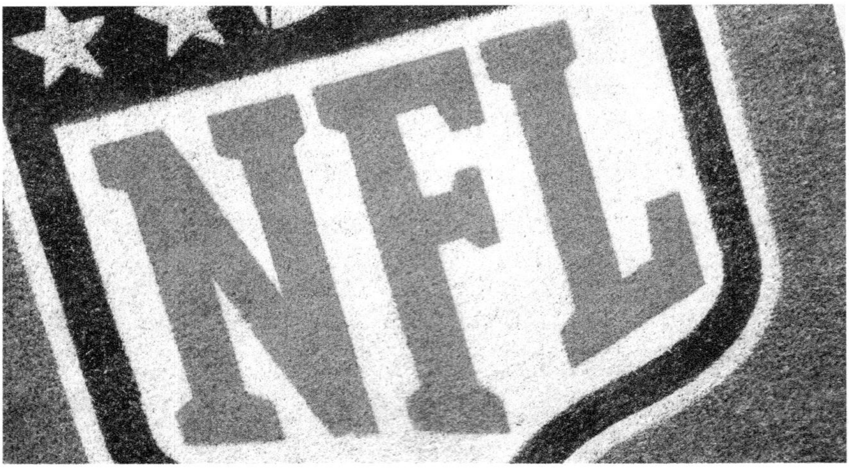
NFL

CHAPTER ONE
TERMINOLOGIES OF AMERICAN FOOTBALL

Listening to commentators call an NFL football game for the very first time may appear like listening to monkey gibberish until you understand basic football language. Understanding the slang and jargon that sum up as a lingo for American football is what makes it enjoyable.

Official Terms

Back judge (BJ): The back judge concentrates on players on the defensive and offensive lines. The back judge, who typically lines up approximately 25 yards downfield on the tight end's side of the defensive backfield, counts defensive players, maintains track of the game clock, and counts all commercial breaks.

Backfield: The group of offensive players, which consists of the quarterback and the running backs, who are positioned behind the line of scrimmage.

Center: The player, who lines up in the center of the offensive line, snaps the football through his legs to the quarterback to open each offensive play. He is in charge of instructing his offensive linemates on who to block.

Chain crew: Eight members of the home team work for the officials, who utilize a 10-yard chain between two posts to keep track of where the ball should be placed and where a team must advance to get a first down.

Cleats: The standard "sneaker" style footwear that players wear during games. For each game, teams choose a color, usually black or white, and all participants are required to wear that color. A player may choose to wear a shoe brand and style that the league has allowed, or he can choose a different shoe as long as it matches the color of his teammates' footwear. Kickers and punters are not allowed to modify their footwear to gain unfair advantage when kicking the football.

Coin toss: In the coin toss ritual, each team may have up to six captains (inactive, active, or honorary); however, only one captain from the visiting team (or a captain chosen by the referee if there is no home team) may declare the coin's selection. The winning team may then have just one captain reveal their choice.

Cornerback: Cornerbacks play across from wide receivers in a defensive backfield. Two cornerbacks make up a typical defensive setup.

Dead ball foul: A foul committed between the time a play is whistled dead and the ball is snapped for the subsequent play, or a taunting foul committed at any time.

Dead ball: Whenever play is stopped, whether it is for a down or a timeout, the ball is deemed "dead."

Defensive backfield: The area where linebackers and defensive backs are lined up on the defensive line of scrimmage. The term describes the defensive "backs" that are positioned in that part of the field.

Defensive end: Defensive ends strive to force their way into the offensive backfield while positioned at the outside ends of the defensive line in order to pressure or sack the quarterback or stop the running back.

Defensive tackles: Defensive tackles, who are often positioned on the defensive line across from the guards, press into the offensive line in an effort to disrupt or halt a play in the opposing team's backfield or to impede the offense from getting yardage on running plays. A 4-3 defense consists of three linebackers, four defensive linemen, and two defensive tackles.

Down by contact: When a player with the ball touches the ground with any part of his body other than his feet, hands, or arms as a direct outcome of hit or contact with a member of the opposite team, that player is judged "down by contact". Any player who touches the ground with a body part other than his feet, hands, or arms and receives no contact from a defender is allowed to get back up and move the ball. The only exception is when the ball carrier voluntarily stops moving forward, kneels down, or gives himself up.

Down judge: The down judge controls the line of scrimmage, oversees the chain crew, and keeps an eye out for penalties for encroachment and offside. The down judge, who is positioned on the sideline across from the press box, counts the offensive players present on the field, evaluates sideline plays on one half of the field, and notifies the referee of the current down.

Down: Downs are the fundamental unit of measurement in American football. The team in possession (the offense) has four attempts to advance 10 yards and earn a "first down" in order to maintain possession of the ball. Consider the following scenario: The New York Giants are playing the Washington Commanders, and they gain possession of the ball on their 36-yard line. To maintain possession, they must move the ball 10 yards to the 46-yard line. If they do, the Giants receive four more downs to advance the ball at least 10 yards to the 44-yard line of their opponent (46 to 50 is four yards, and then it counts down from 50 to 44). The Giants would then be in "territory" of their rivals. An announcer would likely state, "The Giants hold the ball inside Washington territory at the 44-yard line."

Downfield: The region of the field where the offensive team runs plays to gain yards with the ultimate goal of making a touchdown or a field goal. This region is located between the line of scrimmage and the end zone.

Drive: The series of plays that take place when the offense is in possession of the ball, ending when they punt, score, or give the ball to the other team.

Encroachment: A defensive penalty for entering the neutral zone, where players line up before the snap, by a defensive player

End lines: The lines that delineate the field's boundaries at either end, behind the end zone. These lines are ten yards past the goal lines and perpendicular to the sidelines.

End Zone: Each end of the field has a 10-yard zone. When you have possession of the football and are in the opponent's end zone, you score a touchdown. If you are tackled while carrying the ball in your own end zone, the opposing team earns a safety.

Extra point: A one-point kick (also known as a PAT-point after touchdown) that is normally attempted following each touchdown is worth one point. After being snapped to the holder, the ball is often kicked from inside the 10-yard line, either from the 2-yard line (in the NFL) or the 3-yard line (in high school and college). It must sail through the uprights over the crossbar of the goalpost to count as a score.

Fair catch: A motion whereby the punt returner moves his outstretched arm over his head while waving it in front of him. A player cannot run with the ball after indicating for a fair catch, and those intending to tackle him cannot touch him.

Field goal: A three-point kick that can be made from anywhere on the field; however, it's often made within 40 yards of the goalpost. Similar to an extra point, a kick must go over the crossbar and drop between the uprights of the goalpost to be considered successful.

Field judge (FJ): The field judge looks for illegal use of hands and blocking fouls on the receiver who is split widest on one side of the field, as well as penalties on the defensive back who is covering him. The field judge, who is positioned 20 yards downfield on the same side of the field as the line judge, is positioned in the defensive backfield and counts the number of defensive players on the field in addition to keeping an eye on the sidelines to determine if runners are in or out of bounds.

Fourth down: This particular down demands extra attention because realizing it will make the game more enjoyable for you. Let's say it is now fourth down and the offense has not advanced the ball 10 yards. Big deal? Yes, a major issue. The offense can attempt to gain the last few yards necessary for a first down, but doing so comes with danger. Here, there are two important elements. First off, it's a hard shot to gain that many yards in a single play if the offense has been pushed back and has actually lost ground on its set of downs, Let's say it's fourth (down) and 18. Field position is another important consideration in a fourth-down situation. Say you are in opponent territory at the 20-yard line (your opponent's end of the field). If you fail to gain a first down, your opponent gains control of the ball. It's a terrifying position because they just need to advance the ball 20 yards to score. What do you do then? Check *Punt*.

Fullback: The fullback, who is usually the bigger of the two running backs positioned behind the quarterback, frequently acts as an additional blocker for the halfback or tailback on running plays. Although fullbacks often carry the ball when a strong running style is required, such as when the offense just has to gain a few yards for a first down or to score a touchdown,

Fumble: Loss of ball possession while sprinting with it or getting tackled. A fumble can be recovered by both the offense and the defense. A fumble is referred to as a turnover if the defense successfully recovers it.

Handoff: The act of passing the ball to a player. Handoffs are typically exchanged between a running back and the quarterback.

Hash marks: The lines in the center of the field that represent one yard on the field. Before each play, the ball is spotted between or on the hash markers, depending on where the player with the ball was tackled on the preceding play.

Holder: The holder is the player who collects and sets the ball (holding it on one end) during place-kick attempts so that the placekicker can attempt a field goal or extra point by kicking the ball through the uprights.

Huddle: The coming together of 11 team players on the field to map out strategy between plays. In the offensive huddle, the quarterback calls out the plays.

Incompletion: A forward pass that is attempted but is unsuccessfully caught by a receiver, or a pass that falls off or is caught out of bounds by a receiver.

Ineligible receiver: A player who is not allowed to legally receive an advance pass. Included in this are offensive players who are not lined up for a play at the offensive line's center or at least a yard behind it when the ball is snapped. Unless they report as eligible to the referee, offensive players wearing numbers 50–79 are ineligible. An eligible receiver who moves out of bounds before or during a pass becomes ineligible, even if he returns inbounds. More on *ineligible receivers* in *Chapter Three*

Injury timeouts: An official may declare an injury timeout in order to allow an injured player to leave the field and receive medical assistance. If it seems like a player is hurt and attempting to continue playing, Independent Certified Athletic Trainers, known as ATC spotters, have the authority to halt the game.

Interception: A pass that is caught by a defender, ending the offensive team's control of the ball.

Kickoff: A free kick that brings the ball into play and cannot be attempted to be blocked by the side receiving it. A kickoff is used to begin the first and third quarters, as well as after each touchdown and successful field goal.

Lateral: A pass that is made backwards or sideways. Contrary to forward passes, laterals can happen anywhere on the field so long as they don't travel forward, and a team is allowed to do laterals as often as it wishes on any play.

Line judge (LJ): The line judge monitors the line of scrimmage for encroachment and offside. The line judge counts the offensive players on the field and makes decisions regarding plays near the sidelines on half of the field while being positioned on the sideline opposite the down judge and gazing down the line of scrimmage.

Line of scrimmage: An imaginary line that spans from the end of a play to the two sides of the football field. Neither the defense nor the offense can cross the line until the ball is snapped to play.

Linebacker: Linebackers, who are positioned between 3 and 5 yards behind the defensive linemen, assist the linemen on rushing plays by halting the runner. They can also drop back into pass coverage on passing plays or pressure the quarterback.

Loss of down: When an offensive team commits certain types of penalties, the offense loses the opportunity to restart the down and is penalized with a yardage penalty. For instance, if this kind of violation occurs on first down, the yardage penalty will be applied, and the play after that will be on second down.

Muff: When a player makes contact with a loose ball while seeking but failing to regain possession. Muffs typically happen when a kick or punt returner is unable to make a proper catch on a punt or a free kick.

Neutral zone: A virtual area that, after the football has been set up for play, runs from sideline to sideline and is defined by its forward and backward points. The neutral zone is divided into the offensive and defensive lines, and no team is allowed to enter it until the next play is signaled.

No-huddle offense: when the offensive team does not huddle before lining up to run a play. This is either done to save time or to surprise the opponent and keep the defense from making substitutions.

Nose guard/nose tackle: The nose guard, who is positioned on the defensive line opposite the center, pushes into the offensive line in an effort to impede or stop a play in the opposing team's backfield or prevent the offense from gaining yards on running plays. Only a 3-4 defense, which consists of four linebackers and three defensive linemen, uses a nose guard.

Offensive backfield: The area just behind the offensive line where the offensive line's running backs and quarterbacks are lined up. The term describes the group of offensive "backs" that line up in the field's center, including the quarterback, running back, halfback, and fullback.

Offensive guard: On the offensive line, two guards stand to each side of the center and attempt to either open up channels for the running back on rushing plays or block approaching pass rushers on passing plays.

Offensive line: Five men form a human barrier to guard and protect the ball carriers and the quarterback. Each line consists of a center (who snaps the ball), two tackles, and two guards.

Offensive tackle: Outside of the guards, two tackles are lined up at both ends of the standard offensive line formation. On passing plays, tackles defend the quarterback by preventing the pass rushers of the opposition, while on rushing plays, they work to create space for the running backs.

Offside: Before the ball is snapped and enters play, a player is considered offside and incurs a five-yard penalty if any part of his body is within the neutral zone or past the line of scrimmage.

Out of bounds: If a player touches a boundary line or anything on or outside of one, other than another player, an official, or a pylon, he is out of bounds.

Penalty: A player or team who is found to have violated the rules of the game will be punished. These could take the form of a down loss or a yardage penalty. An official will toss a yellow flag onto the field after calling a foul.

Pitch: A long, underhanded pass from the quarterback to the running back during a running play, usually with both hands.

Place Kick: The act of kicking a football while it is being held still and upright, either by the "holder" or a tee.

Placekicker: A player with a specific role who enters the field to attempt field goals, extra points, and kickoffs. Alternatively, a team could have a stronger-legged kickoff expert who kicks the ball deep downfield on kickoffs and a more accurate kicker who kicks the ball through the uprights.

Pocket: The free space that the quarterback's offensive line creates around him to stop a defensive player from sacking him.

Punt: A kick executed when a player lowers the ball and kicks it as it drops towards the ground. A punt is typically executed on fourth down when the offense is forced to give up ball possession to the defense due to a failure to advance 10 yards. Say you are in opponent territory at the 20-yard line on a fourth down, the offense will decide to punt in order to deny the opposition an easy way to potentially score. The ball is snapped to a skillful punter, who kicks it as far downfield as possible.

The opposition player who receives the punt is then attempted to be tackled by the punting team before he can gain any yardage. Often, the person preparing to catch a punt will raise his right hand to signal a fair catch if he notices a group of opposing players racing dangerously at him. If he does, he is protected from being tackled, and the ball is spotted where he caught it. Okay, so you failed to obtain a first down in your four efforts, but at least a strong punt would give the other team a large field to cover for them to score. At this point, the announcer will likely remark something like, "The Giants left themselves in great field position with that punt."

Punter: A member of the special teams who enters the game on fourth downs in order to kick the ball towards the end zone of the opposing team when his team is unable to gain enough yardage for a first down and is too far from the goal posts to aim at a field goal.

Quarterback: The quarterback is the player who serves as the offense's coordinator, gathers his teammates, and calls out the plays to be run. He takes the snap from the Center during a play and attempts to move the ball into his opponent's end zone by carrying it himself, giving it to a running back, or successfully completing a forward pass to a wide receiver.

Red zone: The unofficial zone that extends from the opponent's 20-yard line to their goal line. In any situation around this zone, the defense considers it a moral triumph if it can limit the opponent to a field goal.

Return: Catching a kick or punt and sprinting in the direction of the other team's goal line with the objective of scoring or making significant advances in yardage.

Runner: Any player attempting to advance the ball toward his opponent's goal line while in possession of it.

Running backs: Running backs, often known as halfbacks or tailbacks, are usually the primary ball carriers and the quicker of the two backs set up behind the quarterback in a standard formation. On an offensive play, he has the option of carrying the ball himself or catching a forward pass.

Rushing: To carry the ball forward instead of passing it. A rusher is another name for a running back.

Sack: When a defender brings down the quarterback (while still holding the ball) behind the line of scrimmage.

Safety: A score that the defense scores if he tackles an offensive player with the ball in the defender's own end zone. This score is worth two points.

Secondary: the four defenders who stand against the receivers on the field's sides and behind the linebackers to intercept passes.

Shift: The simultaneous movement of at least two offensive players prior to the snap.

Side judge (SJ): The side judge backs up the official clock operator and acts as the main timekeeper if there is a clock failure. The side judge, who is positioned 20 yards downfield in the defensive backfield on the same side of the field as the head linesman, counts the defensive players present and also alerts the referee when time is up at the close of each quarter.

Sideline: The area where, on game days, league employees, medical and technical staff, and players who aren't currently participating in the game work.

Snap: The act of the Center hiking (throwing the ball between the legs) to the Quarterback, holder on a kick attempt, or Punter. The moment a snap occurs, play has officially started.

Special Teams: The 22 players on-field for kickoffs and punts These teams feature special punt and kick returners and kick and punt coverage specialists.

Spot of enforcement: Where the ball is placed by the referee to establish the line of scrimmage for the subsequent play following the addition or removal of penalty yards from the preceding play.

Tackle box: The zone of the offensive backfield situated in between the two offensive tackles that are positioned at either end of the line of scrimmage.

Tackle: A defensive player makes a tackle when they push the ball carrier out of bounds or to the ground to halt the play and stop the runner from advancing down the field.

Tight end: A tight end positions up on the offensive line's outside of the tackle and can either serve as an additional blocker for rushing plays or switch to a receiving role for passing scenarios. Although certain offenses call for two tight ends, the traditional formation only uses one.

Timeout: A game may be legitimately stopped at any point by one of the sides or by a referee. In each half of a game, each side is given three timeouts, which they can use to tactically stop the clock. When measuring first down yardage, if a player is hurt or if an unintended delay is using up playing time, officials may also decide to call timeouts.

Touchback: A scenario in football where the ball is down behind the goal line after a kick or an intercepted forward pass, and is then put in play by the team defending the goal on its own 25-yard line.

Touchdown: A six-point scoring opportunity that arises when a player with the ball crosses the opponent's goal line, catches it in the opponent's end zone, or recovers a lost ball in the opponent's end zone during a defensive play.

Turnover on downs: The ball is turned over "on downs" and the opposition side takes possession of it, where in the previous play the offensive team failed to accumulate enough yards to earn a first down and another set of downs.

Turnover: When the offensive team loses the ball—often through a fumble or an interception—and a defensive player recovers possession of it.

Two-point conversation: A team may elect to score two points following a touchdown by running a single play from the defense's two-yard line rather than kicking an extra point.

Similar to scoring a touchdown, the two-point conversion is successful if the ball crosses the goal line or is caught in the end zone.

Umpire: The umpire keeps control of the line of scrimmage by keeping an eye out for holding and blocking violations. The umpire, who stands about 10–12 yards behind the line of scrimmage opposite the referee, also inspects players' equipment, counts the number of offensive players on the field, and calls penalties.

Wide receiver: Wide receivers line up closest to the sidelines on either side of the offensive line, sprint downfield, and receive throws from the quarterback. They are renowned for their speed and catchability. Two wide receivers are required in a standard formation; however, some offenses deploy three or four wide receivers simultaneously.

Yard lines: The marks on the football pitch that are used to measure distance. Yard lines are marked every five yards parallel to the goal lines.

Slangs and Nitty-gritty

Audible: When a quarterback switches the play that was first called in the huddle for a different one at the line of scrimmage.

Hail Mary: A lengthy toss that a quarterback often throws to several receivers in an attempt to score a touchdown. It usually occurs at the conclusion of games or halves as a desperate attempt by a team that is trailing to tie the game or win it. Although the phrase had been used in football slang since the 1930s and refers to a Catholic prayer, it gained recognition in 1975 when Dallas Cowboys quarterback Roger Staubach said after throwing the game-winning touchdown pass to wide receiver Drew Pearson, "I closed my eyes and said a Hail Mary."

Hard count: A method by which quarterbacks advise the center when to snap the ball by altering their audible snap count in an effort to force defensive players to unintentionally cross the neutral zone and, as a result, shift the offense five yards forward as a result of a penalty.

Hurry-up offense: When an offensive team decides to run a series of plays without huddling to talk. The goal is to run as many plays as you can in the shortest period of time possible, which is typically employed when running out of time.

Icing the kicker: Calling a timeout just before the kicker for the opposite team is ready to make a crucial kick. The strategy is used in the hopes of upsetting the kicker's timing and planned method. According to the argument, the extra time will increase the pressure on the kicker to think through the situation's potential consequences.

In the trenches: The line of scrimmage is where the defensive and offensive linemen square off shortly after the ball is snapped.

Locker room guy: One who is essential to the team's success, both on and off the field, even if they don't necessarily play in every game, by offering moral support. The added experience, which is frequently provided by an older player, keeps a team motivated after a win or helps them bounce back from a loss.

Nickelback: A defensive formation used when the offense is anticipated to pass. To cover opposing wide receivers, a fifth defensive back is frequently added to the field at the expense of a linebacker.

Onside kick: A kickoff that is purposefully shortened in the hopes that the team doing the kicking will keep possession of the ball. Typically employed by trailing teams at the final moments of games.

Pick-six: An interception that is returned for a touchdown.

Pigskin The football's nickname. The moniker is said to have originated from the legend that the first footballs were constructed from an inflated pig's bladder covered in durable leather, maybe pig hide. These days, cowhide is used to make them.

Pooch-kick: When a kicker purposefully decides not to launch the ball with all of his or her weight in order to prevent a potential comeback by a deadly returner. The ball frequently lands short and in and around blockers who hardly ever touch a ball throughout the season, much less during a game. Typically utilized at the end of halves or games, the offensive team gives up yardage in the hopes of clinching a victory.

Shotgun: When the quarterback chooses to take the snap farther from the center.

Victory formation: The quarterback of the team will instantly kneel after the snap to let time pass when trying to cling onto a lead and run down the clock. Typically used by the winning side at the final moments of halves or games.

CHAPTER TWO
THE BASICS

Equipment

Helmet: includes jaw padding, a built-in face mask, a chin strap, a mouth guard, and specific shock absorbers to lessen the force of ball strikes. Helmets come in different designs based on the position of the player on the field. Some facemasks provide more protection, while others provide a wider vision area.

Shoulder pads: A piece of equipment that has a strong plastic outer shell and shock-absorbing foam interior to give the players broad shoulders. Shoulder pads should be purchased based on comfort, quality, and fit. Getting correct shoulder pads requires that there be no movement to the pads when worn, and they should be as tight as possible. The tighter the shoulder pad is to the body, the better protection it will give and the least chance for an injury.

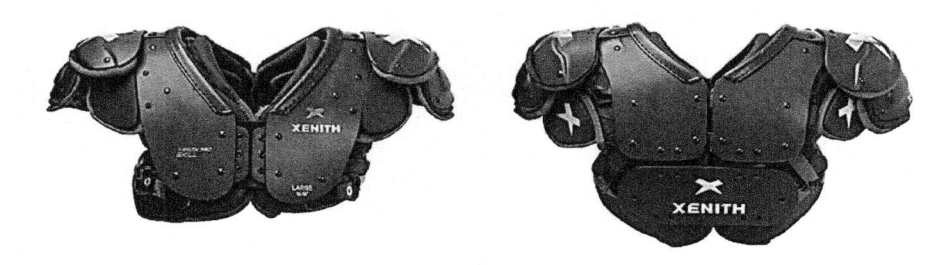

Arm pads: Arm protectors that are light and flexible to keep players from getting bruises

Elbow pads: This protects and detorts impact on elbows with its skin-tight webbings.

Rib pads: The rib pad absorbs and distributes shock by being precisely engineered to normalize player body temperatures and safeguard against injuries.

Hip and Tailbone pads: These are inserted into the belt's pockets, which are worn beneath the pants.

Thigh and knee pads: quilted cushions made of plastic and foam are inserted into the pockets sewed inside the pants.

Gloves: Although hand gloves aren't essential for players, the heavy padding provided by the linen helps to safeguard fingers and hands.

There are basically three types of gloves on the market: high-impact, low-impact, and no-impact. A low-impact glove has padding on the outside but no padding on the inside, which gives you the protection of the outside of the glove but is still flexible for catching footballs or doing a tackle. A high-impact glove is a bigger glove and has protection on the outside and on the inside of the glove. There are two types of material used for gloves: leather and latex. The leather glove has more natural feelings to it, whereas the latex glove has a better grip. However, when you sweat, leather gloves are highly recommended, as the latex glove gets a little bit slippery.

Cleats: Players require proper sole footwear with spikes known as "cleats" beneath the sole made specifically for grass sports. A lot of factors are usually involved when players pick cleats for their position. In other words, the bigger the guy, the bigger the cleats. There are basically three different cuts of cleats: low-cut, mid-cut, and high-top.

The low-cut cleats are mostly for the smaller guys that basically run fast and do a lot of cutting, and they just need to be able to break in and out as fast as possible. They are not worried about support and protection a lot of the time. These cleats are built for speed and have minimal protection.

Next is your mid-cut cleat, which has a little protection based on the kind of material it is made of (fake leather material). It is breathable and still has some flexibility. A mid-cut cleat can be basically worn in any position.

High-top cleats weigh a lot more than the other ones, and that is because they have a lot more protection and stability.

Jersey: All of the players wear a loose-fitting nylon-material shirt with colored side panels. The team color usually precedes the player's name and number.

Pants: A pair of colored nylon mesh pants with four separate pockets on the inside for preserving thigh and knee protection. Hip and tailbone pads are included, as well as a safety belt to keep the pads in place.

Ovoid ball: The play's ball is an egg-shaped, brown ball known as the Ovoid ball. Its circumference at the center measures 22 inches, or 55 centimeters, and its length from tip to tip is 11 inches, or 35 centimeters. The ball is inflated to a pressure of 0.6 to 1.1 atmospheres and weighs around 450 grams.

Order of Play

Football games begin with a kickoff, where the team that kicks off becomes the defensive team and the receiving team takes on the offensive role. The receiving team aims to advance the ball down the field as far as possible before being tackled or running out of bounds by the kicking team. If the ball is caught in the end zone and a knee is taken or the ball is kicked beyond the end zone, it results in a touchback, and the offensive team begins their drive at the 25-yard line.

Each offensive possession consists of four plays, or "downs," to gain 10 yards. If the offense successfully gains 10 yards, it resets the downs, providing another four chances to advance another 10 yards. The teams line up on opposite sides of the line of scrimmage, an imaginary line that separates the offense from the defense. The center snaps the ball to the quarterback to initiate the play, who can either hand it off for a running play or pass it to a teammate for a downfield advance toward the end zone.

The primary objective of the defensive team is to prevent the offense from gaining 10 yards in four downs by tackling ball carriers, disrupting passes, intercepting passes, or causing fumbles. If the offense fumbles and the defense recovers the ball, they can attempt to advance it towards their end zone for a change in possession or a potential touchdown.

If the defense succeeds in stopping the offense from gaining the required 10 yards, the offense can either punt the ball to the opposing team on fourth down or choose to "go for it", attempting to achieve the remaining yardage through a passing or running play. However, if the offense opts to go for the remaining yardage on fourth down and fails to obtain it, the opposing team takes possession of the ball at that spot.

On fourth down, the offense also has the option to attempt a field goal if they are close enough to the end zone to score three points. The ball changes possession in several scenarios, including when the offensive team attempts a field goal, fails to convert on fourth down, or scores a touchdown (followed by an extra point or two-point conversion attempt).

The winner of the game is the team with more points when the game clock expires. In the event of a tie at the conclusion of the fourth quarter, overtime typically ensues.

Field Dimensions

Football games are played on grass or turf fields that are measured in yards. A comprehensive diagram of how an NFL field is measured is shown below.

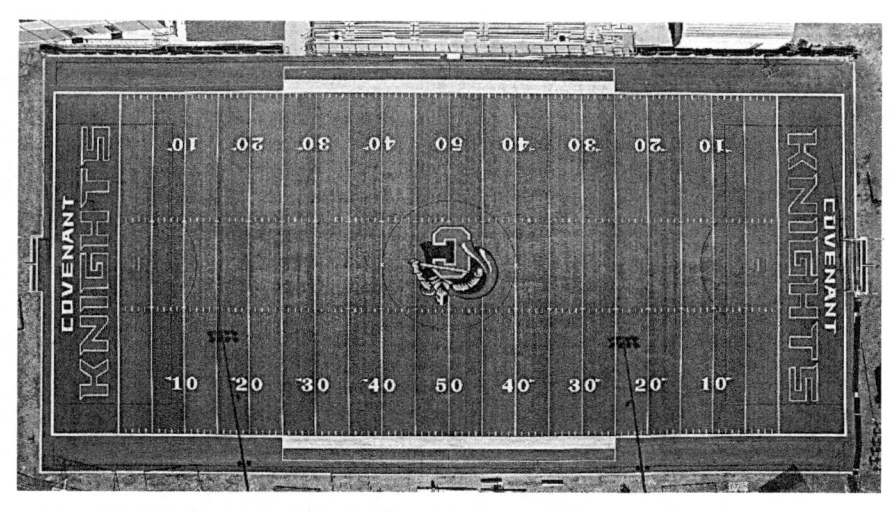

Field Dimensions	Yards
Length of full field	120
Distance from end zone to end zone	100
Width of field	53.3
Size of each end zone	10

NFL games are held on fields that are 53 yards wide and 100 yards long. Each set of "downs" takes place across a 10-yard area. If the offense enters the end zone, which is a 10-yard area on either end of the field, it qualifies as a touchdown. Goalposts are located in the back area of the end zone and measure 10 feet high by 18 feet, 6 inches wide.

The number goes down from 50 yards that divides both sides of the field to the zero-yard line, but there is no zero-yard line. There is what is called the goal line; past the goal line in the colored area is the endzone. Endzones are 10 yards deep. The sidelines, which are often thick for visibility sake, indicate the areas that are out of bounds.

Hash marks are the short lines above the numbers that make up the field's length. They are spaced 17.8 yards apart from the sideline for younger athletes. No matter the level, the distance from end zone to end zone will always be 100 yards.

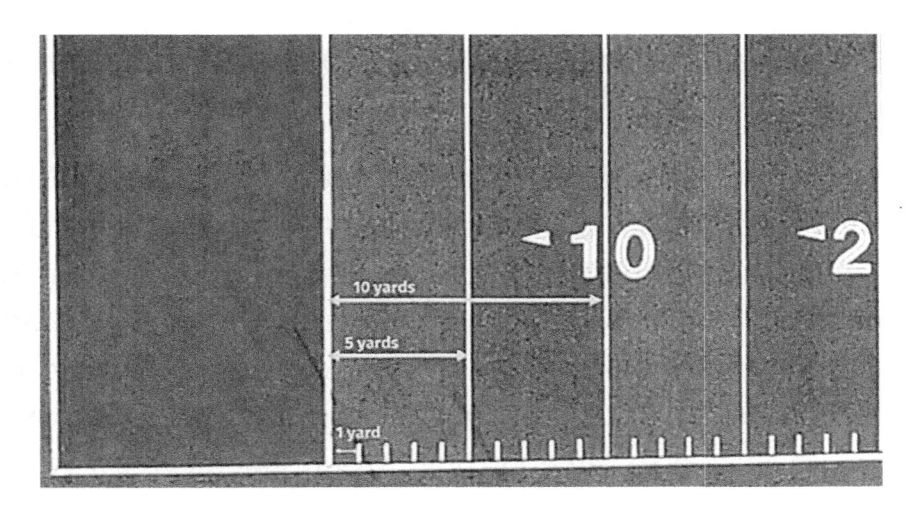

The triangles by the numbers point to the closest endzone, so a player can easily tell which side they are on, even if they cannot see the whole field.

Downs and Yards to Go

One of the most confusing concepts for beginners in American football is the concept of "downs and yards to go". This is a concept that is unique in gridiron football, and it is important that it be understood because on the majority of plays in a game, there will be a down and a certain number of yards to go.

You will often hear two numbers called out during the game; they will be on the screen, and you will probably hear the announcer call them. The first number is what a down is, and a down is really just a chance to move the ball. And a team has four downs to move the ball forward 10 yards, of which, if they are successful, they get another set of four downs to move the ball another 10 yards or beyond. However, if they fail to move the ball 10 yards in four downs, then the other team gets the ball.

Downs were created to keep the ball moving forward. In football's early days, teams would just try to keep the ball for the whole game, so the official body came up with Downs to stop this. It might also seem a little overwhelming for a team to have to move the ball the whole way down the field to score a touchdown. So, by continuously getting first downs, they can make it to the end zone by only gaining a few yards on each and every play.

Let's say, for instance, that a team receives a ball on a kickoff and runs it back to the 20-yard line. This will mean that the first line of scrimmage is on the 20-yard line. At this point, the offense (of that team) will come on to the field and start what is known as a new set of downs. And on the first play, it will be a 1st and 10.

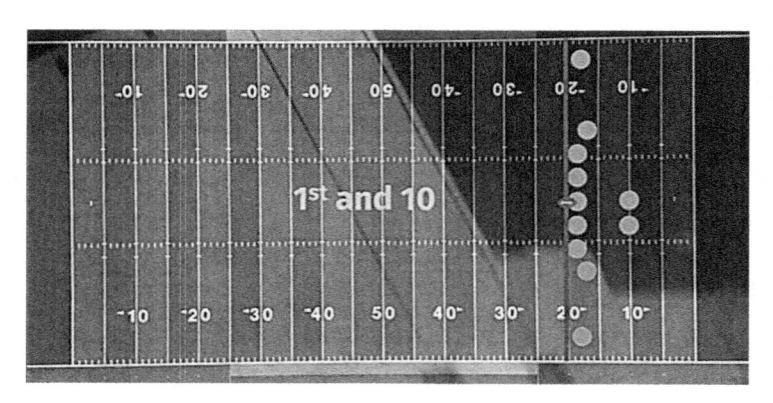

This means that they will get another first down if they can move the ball to the 30-yard line in four plays (downs) or less. If, for instance, they throw a pass and are caught and run up to the 40-yard line, the new line of scrimmage is now the 40-

yard line and becomes 1st and 10 again. But to get another first down from the 40-yard line, they will have to get to the 50-yard line or beyond it.

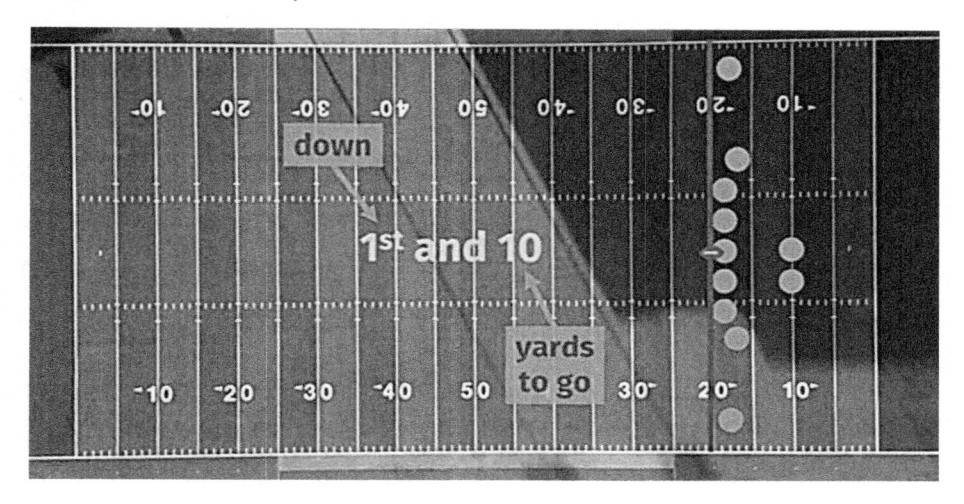

If on the next play they run the ball two yards, a new line of scrimmage is now on the 42-yard line, then they have a 2nd and 8 to go.

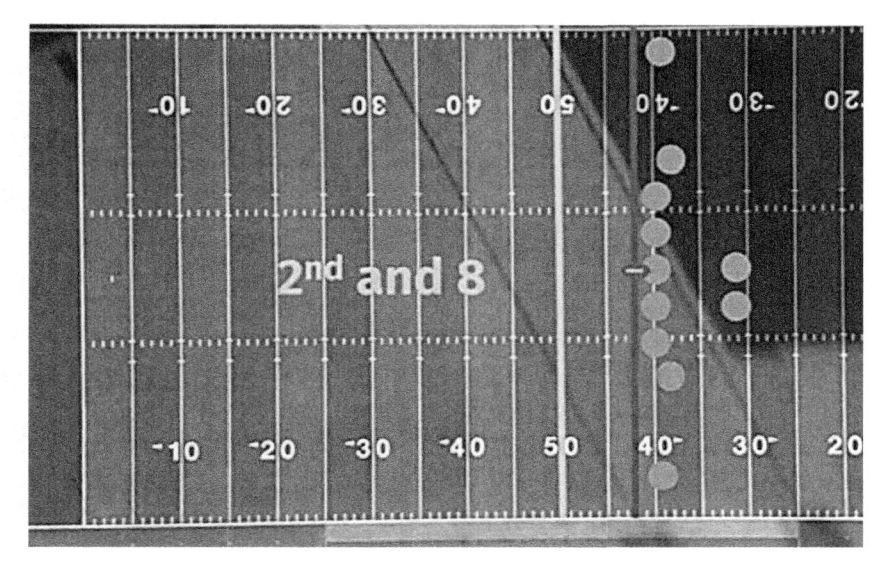

If on the next play they run for 3 more yards, now it becomes 3rd down and 5 yards to go. If they then throw a pass but it is incomplete, they don't gain any yards. Now it is 4th down and 5 yards to go. A team has a few options on 4th downs; they could go for it and try to reach a 5-yard mark or more and get a new first down, but if they fail, the other team will get the ball and start their own first down right at that spot. Another thing to do on a 4th down is punt the ball. The strategy of a punt is basically the offense saying "We are giving the ball to the other team, but let them have it as far down their endzone as possible".

Technically, a team could punt the ball on any offensive play, but you will almost never see it happen before the 4th down. Punting will almost only happen when the offense is in a seemingly disadvantageous position on the field. A team on offense can also attempt to kick a field goal on any play, but like punting, they rarely try one before 4th down. And for a field goal, they also have to be close enough.

Generally, if a team has the ball inside the 33-yard line and they get to 4th down, they will probably try to kick a field goal, which will be a 50-yard field goal attempt. If a team is between a 33-yard and, for instance, a 40 or 45-yard, it is usually too far to go for a field goal, but a punt also will not move the other team back too much; they might actually try to run a play and try to get a new first down. Any yard beyond the 40-yard line, a team will likely punt.

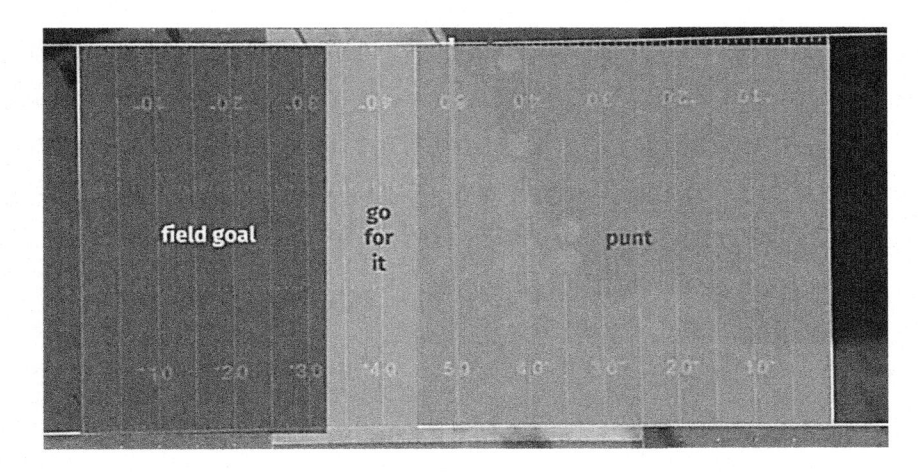

Punting doesn't give a team any points, but it is going to give them a field position advantage. The closer a team is to the other team's end zone, the higher the chance they have of scoring. So, it is to a team's benefit to push the other team back as far as they can.

Watching a game on TV will enable you to catch up on the downs and yards to go quickly, for two reasons. First, there is a down and yard to go for every play except for kickoff, so you would constantly hear the call. Another thing is that on TV now, the lines are drawn on the field.

But if you were to go to games in person, these lines wouldn't be there; however, you can always look at the three orange sticks at the side of the field, which is how the players on the field can tell where they need to get in order to get a first down. They basically show the same thing as the TV lines.

The first orange stick is the original first down, and it is connected with a 10-yard chain to the next first down stick, which shows where they need to get in order to get a first down. The third one will move to a new line of scrimmage on every play, and it shows what Down it is.

Also, for instance, if an offense runs a play and they get the ball down to the six-yard line, meaning there are no 10-yards left on the field to get another 1st and 10. And so if the offense gets a first down inside the 10-yard line, rather than 1st and 10 it is now called 1st and goal.

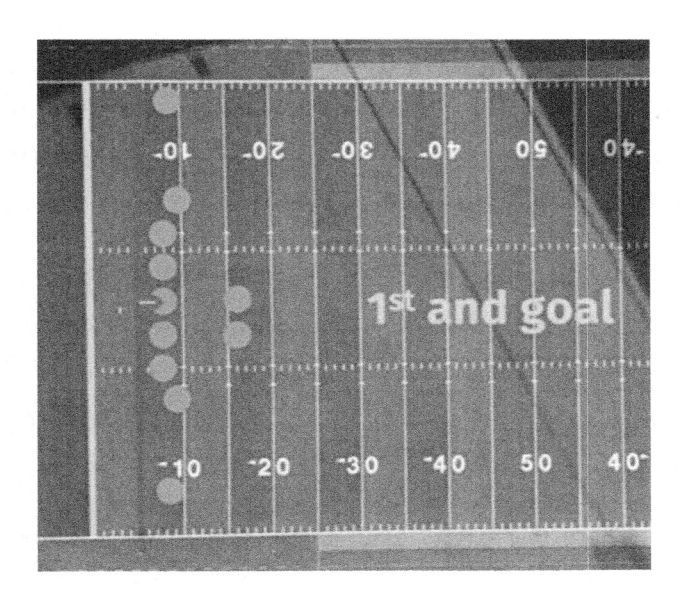

And rather than being able to get another first down, they have four plays (downs) to score a touchdown. And if they fail to get a touchdown on the first three downs, they will probably try to kick a field goal on the fourth down, but not always, because what happens on a third down will often determine if a team is going to get another first down or end up punting on the next play. And that is why there is often talk about third-down conversion rates, which is just a fancy way of saying how many times the offense gets a first down on a third-down play.

Teams will often go for a lot less on 4th down because they risk losing the ball to the other team on that spot, which is why broadcasts often make a big deal about 4th down plays and 4th down conversions as well. Most times, when a team starts a new drive, which means they just got the ball from the other team, and their offense has now come onto the field, they will be able to get at least one or two first downs. Some drives will last over ten plays, but the worst thing a team can do before turning the ball over is to fail to even get one first down, which is called "three and out", since the offense just had three plays and then they were "forced" to punt.

The technical word "forced" to punt is just a figure of speech when it is accepted that a team will punt on fourth down when they are out of field goal range with often a disadvantage position on the field, so it is said that the team is "forced" to punt.

Because of penalties, there are technically no limits on how many first downs a team could get on a drive or how long a drive could last. A penalty will usually result in a loss or a gain of yardage for the offense, depending on which team was the offender. So, if the defense jumps offside on the 1st and 10th plays, they will stop the play, move the ball five yards, and the next play (down) will be 1st and 5 yards to go. On the other hand, if the offense gets a penalty, they could end up with a 1st and 15-yardage to go.

CHAPTER THREE
PLAYERS, POSITIONS AND ROLES

Uniform Numbers and Positions

Football jerseys and over-the-shoulder pads are worn during games. However, these football jerseys are composed of soft nylon and include numbers on both the front and back. Football numbers are important because players must be assigned to a specific number page in accordance with their position. This assists the officials in determining who can and cannot catch the football.

Here are the football number rules:

1-19: Quarterbacks, Running Back, Wide Receiver, Punter, Kicker

20-29: Cornerback, Running Back, Safety

30-39: Cornerback, Running Back, Safety

40-49: Cornerback, Running Back, Tight Back, Safety

50-59: Defensive Line, Offensive Line, Linebacker

60-69: Defensive Line, Offensive Line

70-79: Defensive Line, Offensive Line

80-89: Tight End, Wide Receiver

90-99: Defensive Line, Linebacker

Players and Roles

Every player on the field in football has a specific role and set of abilities. The quarterback, for example, is usually the only one who throws the ball. It is caught by receivers, not offensive linemen. All of these roles must collaborate in order for the coaches' sophisticated plays to be successful.

"Everyone has to be doing their job, and everything has to be in sync," said Craig Karahuta, American Youth Football's vice president of football and cheer operations. "At all times, eleven people [on each team] must do their jobs. "On the field, there is no 'most important' player. That is why, in my humble view, football is the ultimate team sport."

There are basically three teams within a team. A team comes in with 53 players, which are divided into offense (19), defense (19), and special players (15). However, a team can only field 11 players at a time. But the situation in which they are in a game will determine what team is coming on for them.

Offensive Positions

The offense consists of 11 players who team up on running and passing plays to advance the ball into the opposing team's end zone. Once in the end zone, the team can either score a touchdown or settle for a field goal, which are the two most common methods to score in football. These 11 attacking players could come from the following positions:

Quarterbacks

In the majority of football plays, the quarterback assumes a pivotal role, taking the snap from the center and assuming control of the game's direction. During a rushing play, the quarterback may opt to hand the ball off to a running back, while in a passing play, they may choose to pass it to a running back, tight end, or wide receiver. On certain occasions, the quarterback might even decide to run the ball themselves. However, Karahuta emphasizes that excelling as a quarterback transcends merely delivering accurate passes.

According to Karahuta, "a quarterback's responsibilities extend far beyond throwing accurate passes. They must possess an intimate understanding of every player's position on the field. Linemen are tasked with blocking assignments, and receivers must run specific routes. In contrast, quarterbacks need to comprehend the entire landscape of the field, not just their own position. It's a substantial responsibility that demands the ability to survey the entire field comprehensively."

To excel in their role, quarterbacks must be acutely aware of the positions of all players, enabling them to anticipate the whereabouts of their intended receivers before executing a pass. Furthermore, in instances where a pass goes uncaught or is intercepted by the opposing defense, quarterbacks are challenged to display another critical skill: rapid mental recovery.

Quarterbacks must swiftly rebound from their mistakes and regain their composure. This is crucial because they are required to lead their team during the huddle, where the upcoming play is discussed. Also, quarterbacks are tasked with setting the tone for their teammates and guiding them in their respective roles. In essence, quarterbacks must serve as on-field coaches to a certain extent, ensuring that the team operates in a cohesive and effective manner.

Offensive Linemen

With certain offensive positions, the number of players in various positions can fluctuate. While there can be anywhere from one to as many as five wide receivers on the field, there is a steadfast requirement for five offensive linemen. From the quarterback's perspective, these five linemen include the left tackle, left guard, center, right guard, and right tackle.

Notably, the center holds a position of paramount importance within the offensive line. The center is the linchpin of the offensive line. On every single play, the center has a direct interaction with the football. This unique role sets the center apart from any other position on the field. At the commencement of a play, the center initiates the action by snapping the ball and delivering it to the quarterback or another designated player, thus setting the play in motion.

Additionally, the center often assumes the role of captain among the offensive linemen. The center shoulders significant responsibilities when it comes to communication and play-calling among the offensive line. This entails the center analyzing the opponent's defensive formation and making real-time adjustments regarding how the offensive line will execute their blocking assignments. In essence, they determine which opposing players to prioritize, preventing them from reaching the quarterback or running back.

Following the center's snap of the ball, the offensive linemen generally do not engage with the ball again unless specific circumstances arise, such as a tipped pass or a fumble (a situation where a player carrying the ball drops it). In most cases, their primary roles are those of bulldozers, forcibly clearing a path for running plays, or protectors, forming a protective "pocket" around the quarterback to shield him from defensive threats.

Offensive linemen have often been described as "the ultimate teammates" since their mission revolves around enabling their fellow players to excel. By effectively blocking the opposing defense, the offensive line paves the way for running backs to gain crucial yards or quarterbacks to execute successful touchdown passes.

Running Back (RB)
The basic role of a running back revolves around receiving the ball from the quarterback and executing rushing plays. Beyond this, running backs also play a pivotal role in pass protection, shielding the quarterback during certain passing

plays, and they may occasionally venture out as pass-catchers themselves. These athletes are characterized by their remarkable combination of speed and strength, allowing them to shake off would-be tacklers, particularly linebackers. However, it's imperative to recognize that success as a running back hinges on more than just sheer speed.

Vision plays a pivotal role in the skill set of running backs. When in possession of the ball, they do not merely charge forward blindly. Instead, they must discern the optimal running lane and exhibit the agility required to navigate toward it. Situations may arise where the intended path is congested, necessitating a quick change in direction.

Positioned toward the rear of the offensive formation, running backs are often referred to as "tailbacks." Generally, offenses field a single running back at a time, although scenarios can arise with no running backs or even two in certain formations.

Fullback (FB)

A fullback represents a unique hybrid within the realm of running backs, essentially blending elements of an offensive lineman with those of a traditional running back. Typically positioned behind the quarterback and ahead of the tailback within the formation, their primary duty often involves providing blocking support for the running back, who generally serves as the primary ball carrier. This specific role has earned fullbacks the moniker "blocking backs." Despite their primary blocking role, fullbacks are also eligible to carry the ball on occasion, although this occurs less frequently.

You may be curious about the origin of the term "fullback," considering their positioning is not at the farthest rear of the formation. However, this nomenclature has endured from the earlier days of football and is rooted in the sport of rugby, which predates modern football. "Fullback" originally denoted a specific position in rugby, and the term has persisted in the lexicon of American football. In the contemporary pass-oriented era of football, many offenses opt not to deploy a fullback extensively. Instead, they may substitute in an additional wide receiver to better align with the demands of the modern game.

Tight End (TE)

The tight end's positioning on the field is characterized by their close proximity to the offensive line, which explains the "tight" descriptor. These players typically possess greater size compared to wide receivers while remaining smaller than offensive linemen. Their role in the game represents a unique blend of characteristics drawn from both positions.

The tight end serves as a versatile player, encompassing "the strength, power, and blocking prowess akin to an offensive lineman, coupled with the pass-catching and running capabilities reminiscent of a wide receiver." They are tasked with diverse responsibilities, requiring them to execute run-blocking duties akin to offensive linemen, employ spatial awareness to block in open field situations similar to wide receivers, and provide pass protection in line with offensive linemen. Additionally, tight ends must master running routes, catching passes, and advancing with the ball.

Tight ends can be likened to a well-balanced character in a video game, proficient in various aspects without any glaring weaknesses. They possess the capacity to block effectively (though not on par with offensive linemen) and excel at running, catching, and ball-carrying (though not to the extent of wide receivers).

Wide Receiver (WR)
Wide receivers are positioned either directly at the line of scrimmage or in close proximity to it, typically situated on the outer edges of the formation. The "wide" aspect of their position's name reflects their alignment on the field.

While wide receivers may occasionally participate in ball-carrying situations akin to running backs and contribute to blocking on running plays, their primary forte lies in catching passes. They excel in the art of securing passes mid-air, displaying leaping abilities to snatch high throws, and employing adhesive-like gloves to make one-handed catches. Typically, wide receivers are among the fastest players on the offensive unit, often running predefined routes on each play to facilitate the quarterback's targeting.

Another facet of a wide receiver's skill set is deception. Exceptional wide receivers possess the ability to mislead opponents by concealing their intentions, thereby creating uncertainty in the defenders' minds. This deception can involve feints or subtle shifts in movement before executing their intended actions. Such tactics allow wide receivers to gain an advantage, creating additional space to secure the ball and advance after making the catch. Some receivers even employ face shields over their helmets to obscure their eye movements, preventing defenders from discerning where they are looking for the ball.

Defensive Positions

The defense, consisting of 11 men, is on the field to prevent the opposing team's offense from advancing with the ball or making a touchdown. They attempt to tackle the player who is in possession of the ball, intercept passes, or even catch the pass themselves. These roles are played by the defense.

Defensive Linemen
Defensive linemen typically comprise the bulkier players who initiate the play at the line of scrimmage. Typically, a defensive formation features three or four defensive linemen, many of whom place one or both of their hands on the ground before the snap. In contrast to the offensive line, where the outermost players are known as tackles, the interior defensive linemen are referred to as defensive tackles (DTs). In situations where only one defensive tackle is deployed, this player may be designated as a "nose tackle" due to their positioning directly over the center of the ball.

The defensive linemen situated on the edges of the formation are denoted as defensive ends (DEs). Historically, their primary duties included penetrating the offensive line to impede running backs, exerting pressure on the quarterback to hasten their throw, or executing a tackle on the quarterback, professionally known as a "sack."

However, the modern game has necessitated an expansion of the defensive lineman's roles. In contemporary football, these linemen may be required to drop back into coverage to impede receivers, raise their hands to deflect passes, or even cover receivers positioned near the line of scrimmage, extending all the way to the sideline. Given these multifaceted responsibilities, today's defensive linemen are expected to possess a higher degree of athleticism than ever before.

Linebacker (LB)

Linebackers assume their positions behind the defensive line, and the number of linebackers on the field is often contingent on the defensive front. When the defense employs three defensive linemen, it typically features four linebackers, whereas four defensive linemen usually result in three linebackers being deployed. In terms of physical attributes, linebackers typically exhibit a smaller and faster profile compared to their defensive line counterparts.

In earlier times, linebackers were primarily tasked with stopping running backs who had penetrated the defensive line, tackling receivers on short or medium-range passes, and putting pressure on the quarterback to induce hurried throws or sack them.

However, linebackers, like numerous other positions, have evolved to encompass a broader range of roles due to the increasing emphasis on passing in the game. Modern linebackers must possess the capability to cover agile tight ends and even some wide receivers, thereby expanding their coverage responsibilities.

Additionally, linebackers often shoulder significant communication responsibilities within defensive units. In particular, the middle linebacker frequently assumes the role of the "quarterback of the defense." This entails the middle linebacker analyzing the offensive formation before each play, anticipating potential developments, and instructing other defenders on their assignments for the impending play.

Cornerback (CB)

Cornerbacks and safeties collectively constitute the "defensive backfield" or "defensive backs," as they primarily operate at the rear of the defensive formation. Cornerbacks are typically positioned on the outer edges of the defense and are frequently entrusted with the task of covering the opposing team's most skilled receivers.

A cornerback's duties can involve assignment to a specific player or a designated area. When covering a player, the cornerback closely shadows the offensive receiver, endeavoring to prevent them from catching the ball, either by deflecting it or obstructing the receiver's path to the ball. In cases where the cornerback is assigned to cover an area, they defend against any player or pass entering that specific zone. Cornerbacks are typically characterized by their speed and superior coverage skills compared to safeties, making them particularly adept at matching up against wide receivers.

Occasionally, you may encounter the terms "nickel back" or "dime back" when referring to defensive backs. When a defense deploys five defensive backs simultaneously, often by reducing the number of linebackers or defensive linemen on the field, the fifth defensive back is referred to as a "nickel back." This player can be either a cornerback or a safety and is frequently employed when the offense fields an increased number of receivers or is expected to pass more frequently. In situations where there are six defensive backs on the field, the sixth is termed a "dime back."

Safety (S)

Safeties serve as the ultimate line of defense within a football team's defensive structure. Positioned at the rear of the defensive formation, their primary responsibility is to ensure that no offensive player breaches the defense's last line. While safeties are often not as quick as cornerbacks, they excel in their ability to read the game and patrol larger sections of the field.

In most defensive formations, two safeties are deployed: the "strong safety" and the "free safety." The strong safety is typically positioned on the "strong" side of the offensive formation, which is often where a tight end is positioned.

Historically, the strong safety was more inclined toward supporting run defense and approaching the line of scrimmage, while the free safety specialized in pass coverage and patrolling the backfield. However, the distinctions between the two have blurred in the modern game. In contemporary football, both strong safety and free safety are typically adept at performing both roles effectively, reflecting the evolving demands of the sport.

Special Team

The offense and defense do not perform kickoffs, extra point attempts (PATs), field goals, punts, or defense of all four. Special teams are the units that perform these special plays.

Kicker (K): Kickers are specialized players responsible for launching the football off the ground in various scenarios such as kickoffs, field goals, and point-after-touchdown (PAT) attempts, which are commonly referred to as "extra points."

Punter (P): Some punters serve a dual role within the team. In addition to their punting duties, they also assume the role of a holder for the kicker during field goal attempts. Additionally, in specific situations, such as after a safety, where the rules permit a punt instead of a conventional kickoff, these versatile punters may also handle the kickoff duties.

Kick Returner (KR): During a kickoff, the kicker boots the ball downfield, and the player designated as the kick returner catches it before embarking on a run towards the opposing team's end zone. Typically, kick returners are known for their speed and agility, and many of them also play other positions on the team, such as wide receivers or defensive backs. This combination of speed and versatility allows them to make the most of the kickoff return opportunity, aiming to gain valuable field position for their team or even score a touchdown if they can navigate past the opposing players effectively.

Punt Returner (PR): When the punter executes a punt to the opposing team, the player assigned as the punt returner is responsible for catching the ball. In some cases, the punt returner may opt to call for a "fair catch," signifying that they will not attempt to return the ball because they anticipate that the opposing team's special teams will be in close proximity to tackle them immediately upon making the catch.

Alternatively, the punt returner may choose to actively return the punt. Similar to kick returners, punt returners possess speed and agility. They often play other positions on the team, such as wide receivers or defensive backs. Their primary objective during a punt return is to secure the ball and then run in the direction of the opposing team's end zone, aiming to achieve a favorable field position for their team or potentially score a touchdown if they can successfully navigate past the opposition's tacklers.

Long Snapper: The long snapper is a specialized player who serves as a distinct type of center on the football team. Their primary role is to execute a lengthy snap, which involves accurately delivering the ball between their legs to either the punter during a punt or the player who is holding the ball for the kicker during field goals and point-after-touchdown (PAT) attempts. The precision of the snap is crucial to the success of these special team plays, as it sets the stage for the punter or kicker to make the subsequent play. Long snappers are highly skilled at this unique and critical aspect of the game.

CHAPTER FOUR
RULES OF AMERICAN FOOTBALL

Timekeeping

Football games are divided into four quarters of play, each lasting 15 minutes on the clock. However, the actual duration of a game typically extends to around three hours due to the numerous stoppages and breaks that occur during the course of play.

The game clock begins running after the snap of the ball but can stop for various reasons, including:

- **Incomplete Pass:** When a pass is thrown and it is not completed (i.e., not caught by a receiver), the game clock stops.

- **Scoring Plays:** After points are scored, such as touchdowns or field goals, the clock stops to account for the scoring play.

- **Out of Bounds:** The clock stops if a player with the ball steps outside the line in the final two minutes of the first half or the final five minutes of the second half.

- **Timeouts:** Each team is allocated three timeouts per half. When a team calls a timeout, the clock stops, allowing for a break in play.
- **Penalties:** When penalties are assessed, the clock may stop, depending on the nature of the infraction and the game situation.
- **Injury:** In the event of an injury to a player, the clock may be temporarily stopped to provide time for medical attention.

However, in between the second and third quarters, a halftime of 12 minutes is used to allow teams to regroup. If the game is tied at regulation, the NFL has an overtime period of 10 minutes to see if either team can win. If both teams have the same score, the game is considered a tie.

Overtime Rule

Football is one of the few sports where overtime at the college level is drastically different than it is in the professional ranks. The NFL version tries to stay closer to normal gameplay, whereas college alters things a little bit more. For a long time, there was no overtime, and games ended in ties a lot. From 1970 to 1973, there were 29 ties in the NFL, but after a rule change, overtime started in 1974. In that year, a single extra sudden-death overtime period was added, but the league eventually felt the teams who would receive the kickoff to start overtime and simply kick a field goal to win were getting off too easily. So, starting in 2011, they implemented some changes, which have stayed until this moment.

Now, regular-season NFL games that are tied at the end of regulation now go to a single 10-minute overtime period. Each team gets two timeouts; there is a coin toss at the start, and the winning team can choose if they want to receive kickoff or which way they want to go. Unlike at the start of the game, in overtime, the team that wins the coin toss will almost always choose to receive the kickoff. In overtime, both teams will have the chance to have possession of the ball unless the team that receives the opening kickoff scores a touchdown or time expires. In other words, if the team that receives the opening kickoff scores a touchdown, they win. If they score a field goal, the other team gets a chance to have the ball.

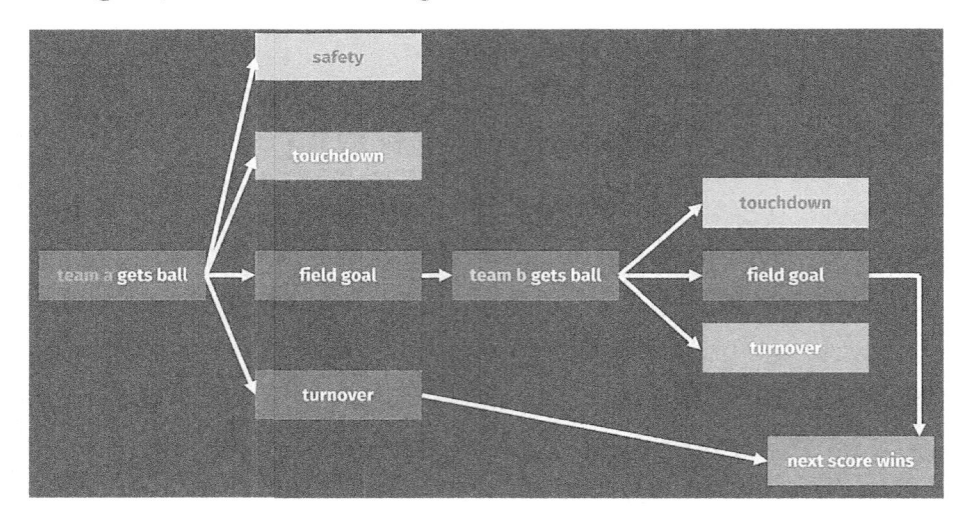

If the second team that gets the ball scores a touchdown, they win. If they fail to score a point either by turning the ball over or turning the ball over on downs, then the team that has the ball first wins. If the second team kicks a field goal and they tie the game, then the game continues, and the next team that scores will win. If the team that receives the opening kickoff turns the ball over before scoring either on downs or with an interception or fumble, the other team will get the ball, and the next team to score will win. The only way the first team could still win on a field goal without giving the other team possession is if they kick that field goal as time expires in overtime.

If the team that kicks the opening kickoff scores a safety on their opponent's first drive, then they will win instantly without ever having the ball. So, time can expire, and a regular-season game will still end in a tie, but in the playoffs, it can't.

Playoffs overtime
Rather than a single 10-minute overtime quarter, overtime in the playoffs basically acts as if a second game is starting. A coin toss will be done, with the visiting team calling for it. Each quarter is 15 minutes, and teams switch sides after the first and third overtime periods. There is a two-minute warning in the second and the fourth, and each team gets three timeouts for every two periods. But the teams will almost never get beyond the first overtime period because the same rule applies to scoring. Each team has to get the ball and complete a drive unless the first team scores a touchdown. There is a slight difference in that the second team to possess the ball either has to score or turn the ball over, including turning it over and down. So, in other words, even if the first team kicks a field goal and time expires on the first overtime period while

the second team is mid-drive, the game will go to a second overtime period to let that team finish their drive, unlike in a regular season where the game will just be over.

If somehow nobody manages to score through four overtime quarters, then they will have another coin toss to start the fifth overtime period.

Play Clock

A play clock governs the amount of time a team has to put the ball in play. A play clock starts after a signal from the referee. In most cases, the play clock is set to 40 seconds following the conclusion of the previous play. During this time, teams can make substitutions, call plays, and lineup in a new formation. After certain stoppages, a team will have 25 seconds to put the ball in play. Beginning with the referee's whistle, the play clock is set to 25 seconds after:

- A change of possession
- A charge team timeout
- Two-minute warning
- The end of a period
- A penalty enforcement
- A try
- A free kick

If the play clock is stopped for any reason before the ball is snapped, the clock will restart with the same time remaining as when it stopped, except in the case of:

- A charged team timeout

- A two-minute warning
- The end of a period
- Penalty enforcement
- Instant replay review

If less than 10 seconds remain on the play clock when it is stopped, the clock will be reset to 10 seconds and start on the referee signal. If the ball is not snapped before the play clock expires, it is a delay of the game penalty and a loss of five yards.

Kickoff Rules

When setting up for kickoff, the kicking team must have at least five players lined up on each side of the ball, no more than one yard from the restraining line.

There must be at least two players lined up between the bottom of the numbers and the sideline. And two between the top of the numbers and the inbound line.

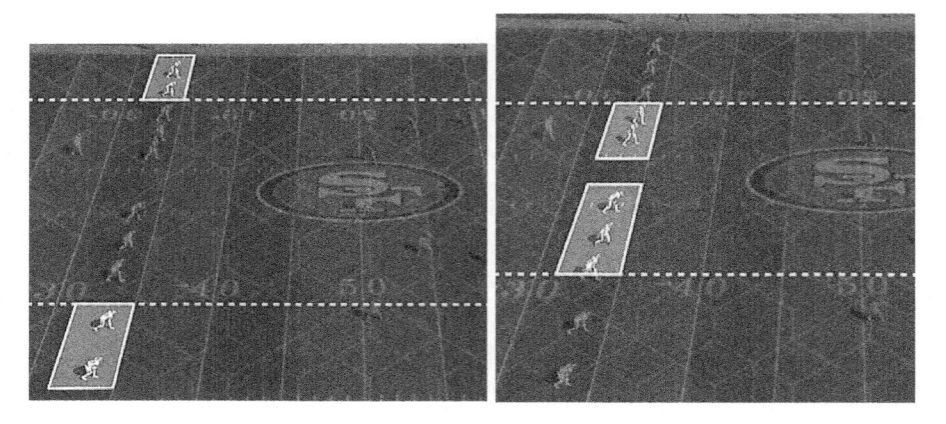

Players on the kicking team may not run down the field until the ball is kicked. The receiving team must have at least eight players in the 15-yard setup zone and no more than three players beyond it.

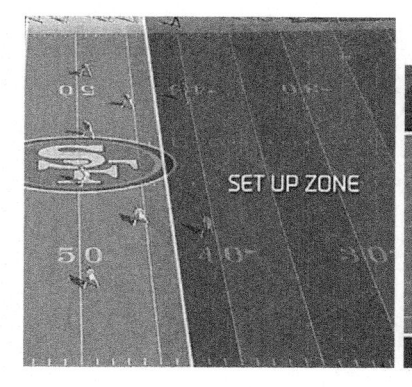

It is illegal for the receiving team to make blocks in the NO BLOCKING zone until the ball is touched or hits the ground.

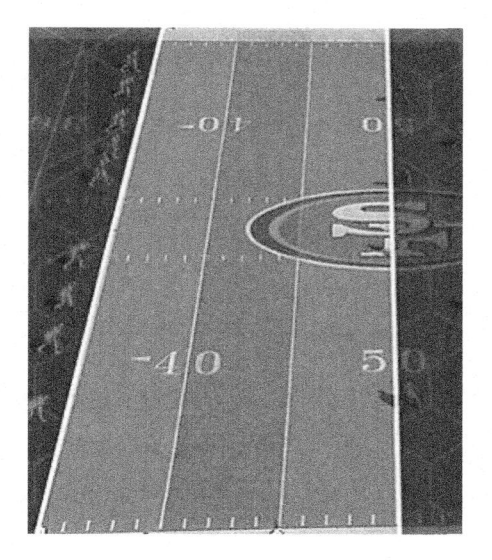

It is illegal for any two players within two yards of each other to initiate a wedge block against an opponent.

It is also illegal for any receiving team player outside the setup zone to engage in a block with a teammate against an opponent.

Freekick Rules

A free kick is a type of kickoff or safety kick used to initiate a play. It must be executed from any point on the kicking team restraining line and within the inbound lines.

1. *Kickoff*: A kickoff is used to start each half of the game, following a PAT, or after a successful field goal. It can be performed using a dropkick or place kick.

Note: The kicking team may use a one-inch-high fabricated tee approved by the League for a place kick on a kickoff. The kicking tee cannot be moved after the ball has been placed on it. If the ball falls off the tee or the tee is displaced, the covering officials will stop play and restart the timing process without penalizing the kicking team. The kicking side must either use a player to hold onto the ball or kick it off the ground if it falls off the tee twice in the same free kickdown.

The ball can be placed on the ground leaning against the tee, as long as the tee remains in its normal upright position.

2. *Safety Kick*: A safety kick is used after a safety is scored. It can be executed through a dropkick, place kick, or punt. The use of a tee is not allowed for a safety kick.

Penalty: Committing an illegal kick on a free kick down results in a loss of five yards.

Restraining Lines

The restraining lines for a free kick are defined as follows, unless they are modified due to a distance penalty:

1. For a kickoff, the restraining line for the kicking team is its own 35-yard line.
2. For a safety, the kicking team's own 20-yard line serves as the restraining line.
3. The receiving team's restraining line is positioned 10 yards ahead of the kicking team's restraining line, regardless of whether it's a safety kick or kickoff.

Freekick Formation

1. **Kicking Team (Team A) Requirements:**

   - Before the kicker approaches the ball and until the ball is kicked, all All members of the kicking team, other than the kicker, shall be positioned no further than one yard behind their restraining line prior to the kicker's approach to the ball and during the entire kickoff period.

- The kicking team must have at least five players on each side of the ball.
- At least two players must be positioned outside the yard-line number and two more must be positioned between the inbound lines and the yard-line number.

Notes:
  - No matter where he is on the field, the place kick holder counts as one of the necessary five players.
  - A player must have at least one foot on the yard line when lining up one yard behind the restraining line.
  - All members of the kicking team, save the kicker and the holder of a place kick, must be inbounds and behind the ball at the moment of the kick.

2. **Receiving Team (Team B) Requirements:**

   - All receiving team players must be inside their restraining line and inbounds until the receiving team kicks or touches the ball.
   - At least eight receiving team players must be placed between their restraining line and a location 15 yards behind their restraining line (known as the "setup zone").

Penalty: For various violations, such as players being beyond the restraining line when the ball is kicked (offside), players going out of bounds voluntarily, or either team being in an illegal formation when the ball is kicked, the penalty is a loss of five yards.

Freekick recovery/catch
   a. A member of the receiving team may advance if he recovers or catches the ball.
   b. If two opposing players are simultaneously in possession of the ball when it is ruled dead, the ball is awarded to the receiving team.
   c. A member of the team that is kicking the ball may legitimately touch, catch, or recover it if:
      - it makes contact with a member of the receiving team first;
      - it approaches or crosses the restraint line of the receiving team.
   d. The ball is dead if:
      - it is recovered or caught by the kicking team's player. If the recovery or catch is legal, the ball belongs to the kicking team at the dead-ball spot.
      - it lands in the end zone with no interference from the receiving team (touchback).
   e. The ball goes dead and belongs to the receiving team at the dead-ball area if it touches down inbounds after crossing the restraining line of the receiving team without being attempted to be possessed by any player.

Notes: A player is deemed to have not touched the ball if it is batted or illegally kicked into him by an opponent. Such touching is ignored, although the bat or kick could be a foul for an illegal bat or illegal kick.

Scoring Rules

Touchdown: In American football, the following are regarded as touchdowns:

1. The football, while in possession of a runner, is positioned on, above, or behind the plane of the opponent's goal line (extended), and the runner has moved from the field of play into the end zone.
2. When an airborne runner carries the football, it must be on, above, or behind the plane of the goal line, and at least some part of the ball must have crossed over or entered inside the pylon.
3. If a player who has control of the ball touches the pylon, it results in a touchdown, with the stipulation that, following any contact with an opposing player, no part of the player's body, except for their hands or feet, makes contact with the ground before the ball touches the pylon.
4. When any player who is legally within the field of play catches or recovers a loose ball that is located on, above, or behind the opponent's goal line, a touchdown is scored.
5. In a rare scenario, the referee may award a touchdown to a team that has been unjustly denied one due to a palpably unfair act.

Conversion: Although it's termed conversion, nothing is actually being converted. The most common conversion is a kick, commonly referred to as a "point after touchdown"

(PAT), a 15-yard play from the defensive goal line. The kicker must shoot the ball between the two upright bars and over the horizontal crossbar. This field goal is worth one point. The side that scores a touchdown can also choose to attempt a two-point conversion running or passing the ball into the end zone from a two-yard line from the defense goal line. This is rarely tried unless it's late in the game because it's significantly riskier than a kick. That extra point can spell the difference between victory and defeat.

Field goal: A field goal in football must meet the following conditions to be deemed successful:

- The kick executed must be either a place kick or a dropkick, administered by the offensive team. It should occur from a position either directly on or behind the line of scrimmage. Alternatively, a fair-catch kick can be performed from the spot where a fair catch is made or awarded. If a fair catch occurs outside the inbound line, the kick's starting point is the nearest inbound line.
- Following the kick, the ball must not make contact with the ground or any player belonging to the offensive team before it successfully crosses the goal. In essence, it must maintain an unbroken trajectory from the kicker to the goal.
- The entirety of the ball must penetrate the vertical plane defined by the goal. This plane extends above the crossbar and between the uprights. If the ball crosses through the goal and subsequently returns through it without striking the ground or any object or person

located beyond the goal, the attempt is considered unsuccessful, although this is rare.

Safety: A safety in American football can occur in various scenarios, and it results in two points being awarded to the opposing team. The primary scenarios in which a safety can be scored include:

- If a player is tackled with the ball in their own end zone, the opposing team is awarded a safety.
- If the offensive team commits a penalty in their own end zone, resulting in a foul, a safety is awarded to the opposing team.
- If the ball becomes dead in the end zone (except as a result of an incomplete forward pass) and the defending team is deemed responsible for it being there (e.g., they fumble or down the ball in their own end zone), a safety is awarded to the opposing team.

Scoring Method	Point Value
Touchdown	6 Points
One-point conversion	1 Point
Two-point conversion	2 Points
Field Goal	3 Points
Safety	2 Points

Penalties

Like in any sport, in football, a penalty is called when a player(s) violates one of the rules that govern the game. If an official has determined that a player has committed a penalty, the official will throw a yellow flag out onto the field. Unlike most sports, in many cases, when a penalty happens, the play is allowed to continue, after which the team that will benefit from the penalty is allowed to accept or decline a penalty based on what happened after the play was run. There are more specific penalties where the official will blow the whistle and stop the play as soon as the penalty occurs. All penalties that are accepted result in the offense losing or gaining a certain number of yards. Most penalties have a certain number of yards that the offense will gain or lose, but there are some that are spot fouls, where the ball will be placed at the spot of the foul for the next play.

To maintain the fairness and integrity of the game, a team of referees is responsible for overseeing various aspects of play. They are tasked with timekeeping, signaling when a player is considered tackled, and enforcing penalties when infractions occur.

Referees carry yellow flags, which they can throw onto the field to signal the identification of a penalty. After the play concludes, the referee will announce the penalty and determine its consequences. Penalties typically result in yards being added or subtracted from the offense or defense's progress, with the specific outcome depending on the nature of the infraction.

There are numerous penalties in the game, so here are the most typical ones.

- *Delay of game:* This penalty is for the offense only. After the ball is set for the next play, the play clock begins to count down in order to pick up the pace of the game. In the NFL, the 40-second play clock starts when the previous down is complete. The offense has to put the ball into play before the play clock runs out or call a timeout. If they fail to do so, the delay of the game penalty is enforced by losing five yards, and the down is replayed.

- *Encroachment:* This is when the defense crosses the line of scrimmage and makes contact before the ball is snapped. This is a dead ball foul; the ball is advanced five yards, and the down is replayed. As long as they return before the snap, a defensive player is allowed to cross the line of scrimmage. However, they may be penalized for encroachment if they make contact with an offensive player while doing so.
- *Face Mask*: A facemask penalty can be called on either team for grabbing the face mask of another player's helmet or pulling and twisting it. Obviously, pulling someone's face mask could lead to a serious injury. And it is a big one because the face mask penalty will cost the team 15 yards.
- *Holding*: This is restricting the opposing player to prevent them from tackling, or who isn't the ball carrier. In broader terms, it is when a player uses his or

her hands and arms to materially restrict the movement of a player who does not have the ball. The details of what constitutes holding are slightly different for offensive players and defensive players, but certain things will almost always be considered holding; these include any sort of grabbing with the hands or wrapping around with the arms, any tugging of the jersey, and any pulling to the ground or tackling of a player that does not have the ball.

However, both sides have different consequences. Holding on the offense will be a ten-yard loss and replaying the down. Defensive holding is a five-yard advantage with an automatic first-down.

- Illegal contact: The officials will flag a defensive player for illegal contact if they initiate any sort of contact with a receiver more than five yards past the line of scrimmage. This includes any form of legal blocking. Illegal contact only applies to defensive players, and it only applies before the ball is thrown.
- *False start*: For the offense only, this penalty is enforced when an offense player moves abruptly before the ball is snapped. The defense is allowed to move all the time, whereas the offense needs to be very still, unless they are in motion when they are placed in their spot. A pesky five-yard loss and a replay of the down follow.
- *Illegal shift*: This is when an offensive player never got set before the snap or when a player never got set before their teammate went in motion.

- *Illegal motion*: This is where the player in motion moves towards the line of scrimmage.
- *Illegal formation*: The offense will be flagged for an illegal formation if players are lined up in a way that violates the rules that govern how they are allowed to line up. The rule demands that at least seven players be lined up on the line of scrimmage. And that will mean that at most four players are to be behind the line of scrimmage. Additionally, the players on each end of the line must be eligible receivers, and everyone in the middle must be an ineligible receiver. An illegal formation comes with a five-yard penalty.
- *Offside*: This is the generic penalty that occurs on a player who is in the neutral zone at the time of the snap. It is a penalty that can technically be called on offense or defense, but it is exceptionally rare for it to be called on offense. Offside is most commonly called on a defensive player who has moved too soon into the neutral zone, but it could also be called on a player who has lined up in the neutral zone. When the defensive player is offside, the play is allowed to continue, and at the end of the play, the offense can choose to accept or decline the penalty. An exception to this is if the player is offside and has a clear pass to the quarterback. Then, in this situation, the play will just be blown dead, because then it is a player-safety issue. This is a five-yard penalty.
- *Neutral zone infraction*: This is where a defensive player is offside, and it causes the offense or someone on the

offense to basically false start. This is a dead ball foul that has a five-yard penalty.
- *Pass interference*: This is a judgment that occurs during a throwing play and can go against the offense or defense. Before the ball arrives at the intended receiver, the defense can't make contact to restrict the player from catching the ball. Offensive pass interference is any contact made by the offensive player on a defensive player that affects the defensive player's ability to catch the ball, e.g., shoving. In the NFL, if defensive pass interference is called, the ball is placed at the spot of the foul, which is an automatic first down. Offensive pass interference is a 10-yard loss from the previous line of scrimmage. With a down being replayed.
- *Personal foul*: This type of foul is called for specific dangerous or unnecessary physical contact. This is a 15-yard penalty.
- *Roughing the passer*: This is any physical act against a passer (i.e., before, during, or after a pass) that the referee judges to be unwarranted based on the circumstances of the play. Roughing the passer occurs when the defender makes late or unnecessary direct contact with the passer after the passer releases the football. Defenders may initiate contact no more than one step after the throw in certain situations. The defender may not perform unnecessary or punishing acts like driving a passer into the ground after the pass. The rule applies even if the hit is not late. It is a foul to

possibly contact the passer's head or neck area, or to lead with a helmet in contacting any part of the passer's body. Or, to hit the knee area or below on a passer, even if the initial contact is above the knee.

A passer who runs outside the pocket area loses the one-step and low-hit protections, but if the passer stops behind the line and resumes a passing posture, he will be covered by all the special protections for passers.

Roughing the passer can be a tricky one because the rules changed a lot just a few years ago, but players now seem to have adjusted, and it doesn't happen as much as it used to. Roughing the passer is the use of excessive force against the quarterback. And this typically occurs when the defense is rushing in to tackle him and he waits until the last second to throw the ball.

Generally, you shouldn't hit the quarterback when he doesn't have the ball, but if you are rushing full speed to try and tackle him, you won't exactly be able to stop your momentum instantly if he lets go of the ball right before you hit him.

This then raises the question: how much time between the release of the ball and the hit is acceptable? This is one of those gray areas that often leads to disagreement on whether a call should or should not be made. It all then boils down to whether the referee judges it to be unwarranted based on the circumstances of the play. Other parts of this include the fact that if a quarterback has thrown the ball, you cannot land on top of him with your full weight. It is also a no-no to ever hit the quarterback in the head. Roughing the passer is a big issue, with a 15-yard penalty and an automatic first down for the offense.

- Roughing the kicker or punter: This is similar to roughing the passer. Field goal and punt plays will often involve defensive players running in at full speed to try and block a kick, which may result in them running into a kicker. Unless the punter really messes up and bobbles the ball, here, the player is trying to go for the ball and not trying to tackle the kicker. The penalty for doing so is a 15-yard penalty and an automatic first down. Although there is also a 5-yard penalty version for less egregious times when a defender accidentally runs into the kicker.
- *Blocking below the waist*: An illegally made block done below the waist.
- *Block in the back*: In football, blocks are to be done from the front.
- *Chop block*: A chop block occurs when an offensive player blocks a defensive player in the thigh or below while that same defensive player is engaged by a second offensive player above the waist.

Chop blocks are illegal on passing plays, kicking plays, and all running plays. On running plays, it does not matter if the chop block occurs on the frontside or the backside; it is still a foul. If the defensive player initiates the contact above the waist, or if it is clear that the offensive player is trying to slip or escape and the contact above the waist is incidental, then it is not a foul.

- *Clipping*: A block done from behind and below the waist. Clipping is illegal outside of the area of close-line play, which is the area between the offensive tackles and three yards on either side of the line of scrimmage. In close-line play, it is legal for an offensive player to block an opponent above the knee. But it is illegal to clip at or below the knee. It is also a foul if a blocker rolls up on the side or back of the leg of the defender after making a block. This rule applies anywhere on the field.

- *Unsportsmanlike conduct*: This involves specific player behavior that the league is trying to remove from the game. This is a 15-yard penalty.
- *Intentional Grounding*: A quarterback may decide to throw the ball away when they are under defensive pressure and in danger of being sacked. It is intentional grounding if they toss the ball in a spot where there isn't a receiver nearby. Penalty: 10 yards, plus loss of down.

Special Situations and Corresponding Calls

❖ If two penalties happen at the same time, one on the offense (holding) and the other on the defense (facemask), these penalties become "off-set" – meaning they cancel out each other, and a down will be replayed with no consequences.

If, however, two penalties happen on the same play by the same team, then the opposing team has the choice of which one to enforce to get a better advantage.

❖ One potentially interesting situation is what could happen if there is defensive interference in the endzone or any foul that will result in moving an offense into the endzone? Do they get a free touchdown? No, they do not. There is no free touchdown in football or any automatic scoring.

❖ What would happen if there was any pass interference committed in the end zone? The ball is automatically placed on the one-yard line, and while it is not a guaranteed score, it is about as close as you can get.

❖ There may also be times when a team is close to the end zone and a foul is committed. Rather than that team getting the usual number of yards, the ball would

be moved half the distance to the goal line from where they are, rather than being placed on the one-yard line.
- ❖ There are also times where the offense can have the ball in their own 10-yard line, and they handoff and are running back rushes for 30-yard, which is a pretty nice gain. But there is a call for defensive holding back at the line of scrimmage. So, if that penalty were to take effect, then they would get 10-yards and an automatic first down from the line of scrimmage rather than the 30-yards that they gained on the play. In this case, the referee will go to the offense and ask, "Do you want to accept this penalty?" And the offense will say "No, we want to decline this penalty". Then the referee will still make his announcement, holding defense number 69, and then say "The penalty is declined". So, as a result of the play, the ball will be placed at the 40-yard line, first down.
- ❖ Holding, as a penalty, could have a lot of gray areas around it. To better understand holding, it is probably necessary to understand what type of blocking is permitted:
    - o If a player does not have the ball, it is legal to perform a block on that player that makes contact with the inside of the player's frame (the torso) or at the shoulders or arms, so long as there is no grabbing, pulling, or anything that creates material restriction
    - o Once the play develops (by a snap) and players are competing with one another for leverage, the

rule book allows players to do things that might have been "holding" otherwise in order to maintain their position against an opponent.

So, there is absolutely a gray area of what will be flagged as holding or what will be explicitly permitted by the rulebook.

Refereeing a football game is no easy task, and mistakes can happen. With the investment in technology, every professional and college game is recorded on camera, thus giving head coaches a chance to challenge particular rulings on the field, not penalty calls. Whether the player caught a pass, if the player really did fumble the ball, or whether the coaches should throw their red flag or handkerchief to challenge the ruling, the cost of these decisions is losing one of their three timeouts. But if the ruling is overturned in their favor (meaning they were right), the timeout is given back to the head coach.

Additional Rules

Ineligible Receiver

The following players are eligible to catch a legal forward pass:

- Any Defensive Player
- Offensive players on either end of the line of scrimmage with eligible jersey numbers (1-49 or 80-89).
- Offensive players who are legally at least one-yard behind the line of the snap.

All other players are considered ineligible receivers unless they first report to the referee the player's position/status on the end of the line or in the backfield. An eligible receiver can also become ineligible if he voluntarily runs out of bounds before or during a pass, even if he re-establishes himself inbounds.

Exception: If he is forced out of bounds by a defender or a foul, he must return to bounds immediately with both feet inbounds. He becomes eligible to receive a pass (without prior touching by another defender or receiver)

All offensive players become eligible receivers after the ball is touched by any defensive player or any eligible offensive player.

Forward Pass

It is a forward pass if the ball initially moves forward towards the opponent's goal line after leaving the passer's hand. The offensive team may make one forward pass from behind the line of scrimmage during each down. When a player is in control of the ball, any intentional forward movement of his hand can start a forward pass. It can be thrown overhand or underhand, one-handed or two-handed.

If contact causes the ball to go backward after the initial forward movement, it is still a forward pass, regardless of where the ball lands. A fumble occurs when the passer loses control of the ball while attempting to return it to his body after intentionally moving his hand forward. It is considered a fumble when the passer drops the ball while re-cocking his arm. The passer must remain behind the line of scrimmage before throwing a pass. If his entire body is beyond the line when the ball is released, it is an illegal forward pass. The defense may intercept illegal passes and advance the ball.

Backward Pass

It is a backward pass if the ball initially travels parallel to or behind the point where it leaves the passer's hand. A runner may throw a backward pass at any time and from anywhere on the field. If a backward pass touches the ground, it is a fumble, and the ball is alive as long as it remains inbounds. If a pass is initially backward, it remains a backward pass even if the ball is batted, muffed, or kicked in another direction while in flight. It is also a backward pass as soon as the ball leaves the hand of the snapper. Some examples include a direct snap from the center, a muffed snap, or a snap that is untouched by any player.

Down by Contact

An official shall declare the ball dead and the down end when a runner is contacted by an opponent and touches the ground with any part of his body other than his hands or feet. The ball is dead the moment a runner touches the ground with any part of his body other than his hands or feet. Any loss of control of the football or forward motion will not count. The placement of the ball for the next down is marked by its location for the time of the dead ball.

A runner may also declare himself down by falling to the ground, kneeling, or clearly making no effort to advance the ball. If a runner slides foot first, the ball is dead until he touches the ground with anything other than his hands or feet. It is a foul for a defender to initiate contact with a runner after they are declared down by contact; such contact will result in a foul for unnecessary roughness.

Defenseless Player

When a player initiates needless contact with another player who is unable to defend himself, it is a foul. There are two types of prohibited contact:

- Forcible contact with the head/neck area with the helmet, facemask, shoulder, or forearm

- Forcible contact with either the crown or the hairline parts of the helmet to any part of the defenseless player's body

Players in a defenseless posture include:

- a player in the act of just throwing a pass
- a receiver attempting to catch a pass

For a passer in the pocket, the legal strike zone is below the neck to above the knee. The legal strike zone for a receiver attempting to catch a pass is below the neck. Players who are considered to be in a defenseless posture also include:

- the intended receiver in the action, during or immediately following an interception
- a runner who is in the grass and whose forward progress is stopped
- a player on the ground

The recipient of a crackback receives defenseless player protection. This is a defensive player in an area five-yards on either side of the yard of scrimmage, and the offensive blocker is more than two-yard outside the tackle when the ball is snapped. If the blocking is from the shoulder to the body, it is legal.

All defenseless players receive protection from an illegal launch. An illegal launch occurs when an opposing player lifts both feet prior to contact and makes possible contact with any part of his helmet to any part of the defenseless player's body.

The following players also receive defenseless player protection:

- A kicker or punter during the kick or during the return.
- A quarterback following a change in possession.
- A kick or punt returner attempting to get the ball in the air.
- The recipient of a blindside block.

- The snapper on field goals and extra point attempts is considered defenseless until he establishes himself in a blocking posture and can protect himself.

When a blocker is moving power-low or towards his own end-line, the legal strike zone is below the neck and above the waist.

In addition to penalties called on the field, violations of this rule (on defenseless) may result in fines and suspensions.

End-zone Fumbling

If the ball comes loose before the runner is down by contact, it is a fumble. Fumbles can occur in the field of play or in the end-zone. If a team recovers a fumble in their opponent's end-zone, it is a *touchdown.* If a player fumbles and causes the ball to go out-of-bounds in his own end-zone, it is a *safety.* If a runner fumbles in the field of play and the ball goes forward into the opponent's end-zone and then out-of-bounds, it is a *touchback* for the defense.

If a fumble falls backwards and out of bounds, the ball is placed in play at the inbounds point by the team that was in possession last. If a fumble falls forward and out of bounds, the ball is placed in play at the location of the fumble by the team that was in possession at the time.

Illegal Peel Back Block

It is prohibited for an offensive player to make side and lower-body contact with an opponent. If the blocker is moving towards his own end line and approaches from behind and from the side, this is known as an illegal peel back block. If the near shoulder of the blocker contacts the front of his opponent's body, the peel back block is legal.

Horse Collar

It is illegal to grab the inside collar of the back or the side of the shoulder pads or jersey and pull a runner toward the ground. This is known as a horse collar tackle, and it is a foul regardless of which direction the runner was pulled towards the ground. If the runner's knee buckles as a result of the tackle or attempted tackle, it is a foul. In addition, grabbing the back of the jersey at the nameplate or above and pulling the runner towards the ground is a horse collar tackle. When a quarterback or runner exits the tackle box or the pocket, the rule takes effect. However, it does not apply to them while they are still there.

CHAPTER FIVE
NFL SEASON SCHEDULING

The NFL regular season kicks off in the month of September and lasts until the end of December. The 272 games schedule is spread out over a span of 18 weeks, where all 32 teams in the league play 17 games each and have a rest day, or what is commonly called a "bye week.". Since each team can't play the rest of the 31 teams in one season like in other professional sports, the NFL has devised a really cool way of scheduling.

Knowing the difference between the conferences and the divisions is a super important part to/ how you comprehend the game. A lot of things stem from this, from the playoffs to scheduling to rivalries.

NFL Divisions

The NFL consists of 32 teams from two conferences, which means 16 teams for each conference: the National Football Conference (NFC) and the American Football Conference (AFC). In these two conferences, the teams are split into four divisions (North, East, South, and West) of four teams each.

Divisions	NFC	AFC
North	Detroit Lions, Packers, Vikings, and Chicago Bears	Baltimore Ravens, Pittsburgh Steelers, Cleveland Browns, and Cincinnati Bengals
East	Eagles, Cowboys, Commanders, and Giants	Bills, Dolphins, Patriots, and Jets
South	Buccaneers, Falcons, Saints, and Panthers	Colts, Texans, Jaguars, and Titans
West	49ers, Seahawks, Rams, and Cardinals	Chiefs, Chargers, Raiders, and Broncos

The matchups are set by a combination of rotation and previous year standings. Within a division, a team will have to play each other twice, once at home and once away. And because teams play each other twice every season (which means they meet a lot), naturally rivalries are going to occur.

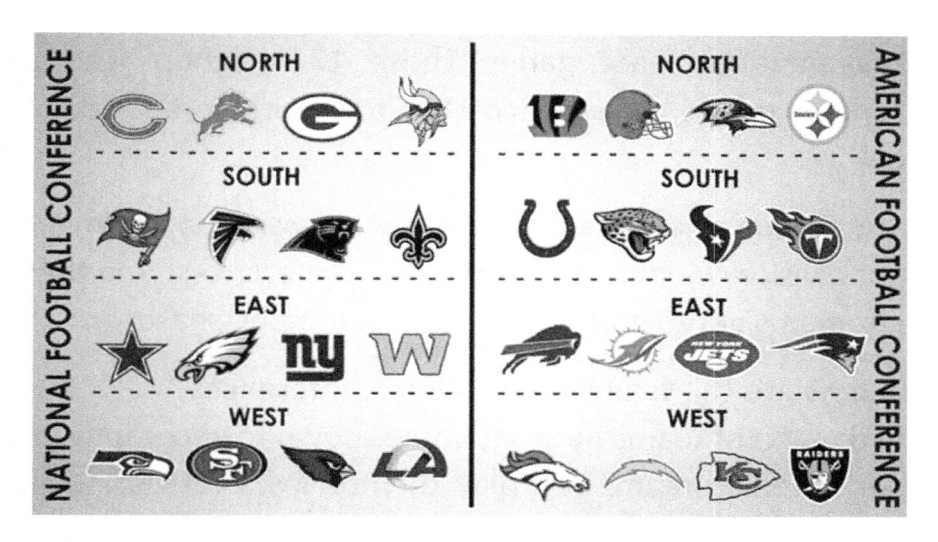

Then every team and that division will play another division in their own conference, two home and two away, which makes it four more games and 10 in total. Next, they will play a division in the other conference in its entirety—two home, two away. Each team plays four games a year against teams in the other conference. An NFC team will only play any given AFC team every four years, and that is only every eight years, since it is being rotated who plays at home and who plays away (on the road).

There are also two more games a team will have to play in their conference by standings. The first-place team in the East will play the first-place team in the South and the West. The second-place will play the two seconds, and the thirds will play the two thirds. That is two more games, which makes it 16. In an expanded season, the same will be done in the other conference (an inter-conference game) against the division that a team is not playing already the present year, didn't play the previous year, and is not playing next year, and that will be a standing space game. These 17 matchups can be arranged in any possible combination within the next 18 weeks.

Every season, there is a winner of each division, which means eight division winners across the two conferences. And these eight teams get to go to the playoffs—the postseason.

But how are the teams divided into conferences?
The division of teams basically comes down to geography and rivalries. Since teams will play themselves a lot during the season, the NFL wouldn't want them to travel too much. In terms of rivalries, for instance, the Greenbay Parkers and the Chicago Bears are old rivals and were obviously kept in the same division - NFC North, and this makes more sense seeing that both of the teams are in the Northern area.

Post-Season

Wildcard
In the NFL, each conference has three wild card teams, totaling six teams that qualify for the playoffs. Originally, there were only two wild card teams per conference, making a total of four wild card teams. However, in 2020, the format was modified to include three teams per conference. A wild card team in football is a team that qualifies for the NFL playoffs without winning its division. They earn this spot by winning a Wild Card round game. In total, there are fourteen teams that make it to the playoffs: eight division winners and six wild card teams (three from each conference). The

selection of the wild card teams is determined using a combination of tiebreakers and win-loss records.

Once a team becomes a wild card team and qualifies for the postseason, they must participate in the first round of the playoffs, known as the wild card round. The matchups in this round are determined as follows: the lowest-ranked division winner in each conference faces the highest-ranked wild card team, followed by the third-lowest division winner in each conference facing the third-highest division winner in each league. The "Conference Champion" of each conference who finishes first in their division receives a bye-week and does not compete in the wild card round.

While it's not common for a wild card team to win the Super Bowl, it has happened on multiple occasions. Wild card teams are typically at a disadvantage in the playoffs because they have to play their games on the home field of teams with higher seeds. Despite this challenge, there have been instances where wild card teams have gone on remarkable playoff runs to compete for and even win the Super Bowl.

The Playoffs

At the end of a regular season, the single elimination postseason begins in early January and ends in February, when the championship game is played, known as the Super Bowl. 14 teams are eligible to play, seven from each conference. The bracket is made up of all four divisional winners and three wild-card teams. The wild-card teams are the three non-divisional winners that have the best overall records in their conference.

From the four divisions of the AFC and the NFC, the top teams from each division automatically go into the playoffs in the top four spots on the side of their conference. In the playoffs, the NFC teams only play NFC teams, and the AFC teams only play AFC teams. And the best team in each of the conferences within the playoffs goes to the Super Bowl.

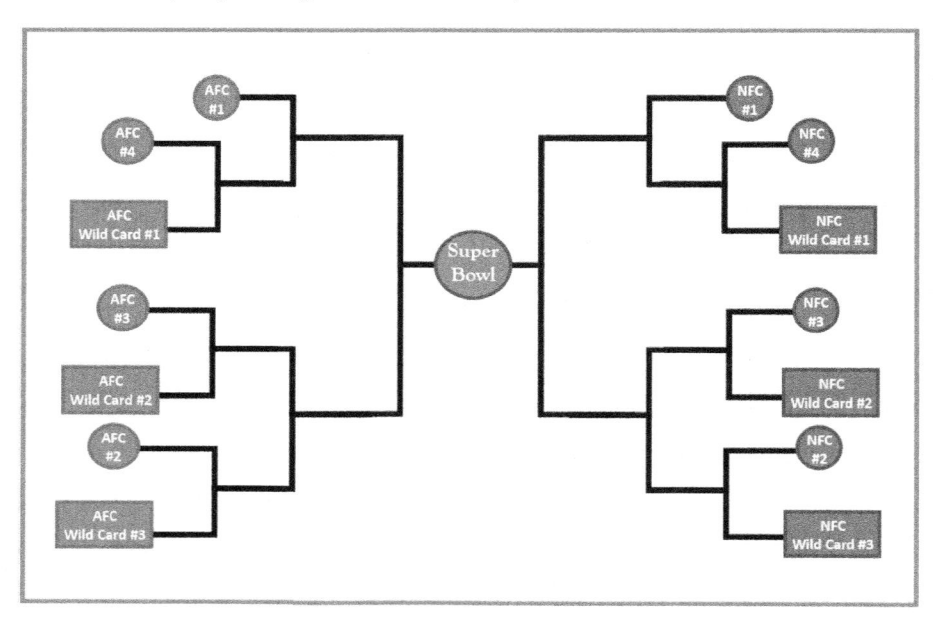

For both conferences, the number one seed will have a "bye week" in the Wild-Card weekend, which means they won't play anyone and immediately advance to the next round, the Divisional Round. For the rest of the teams, the highest seed faces the lowest seed and has a home field advantage – 2 vs 7, 3 vs 6, 4 vs 5. Once the wild-card round is over, there will be three winners per conference out of the three games, plus the number one seed, which will get to host the lowest seed remaining. The other two teams will get to play each other, with the highest seeded one getting home field advantage.

For the conference championship, the two teams remaining from each conference will face each other, and the winners will get to play in the Super Bowl, which already has a predetermined stadium that is independent from the playoff seedings.

The Super Bowl champion receives the Lombardi trophy. It bears Vince Lombardi's name, one of the best NFL coaches ever. The Lombardi trophy is the ultimate prize that each club strives to win each season.

The Vince Lombardi Trophy

The NFL Team that wins The Super Bowl each year will be honored with the Vince Lombardi Trophy and declared the NFL Super Bowl champions. This football trophy is 22 inches tall and is made of sterling silver. The majority of the trophy's body is a long stand, on which the words "Vince Lombardi Trophy" are etched alongside the NFL shield and the year in roman numerals. A regulation-size football caps off the trophy to complete its visual style and give it an instantly recognizable look.

Despite the fact that American football has been played since 1869, the first Super Bowl trophy was given out in 1967 when the Green Bay Packers, under the direction of head coach Vince Lombardi, easily defeated the Kansas City Chiefs in the first Super Bowl. Lombardi also triumphed in the second Super Bowl the following year against the Oakland Raiders.

It is hardly surprising that this head coach would be given the trophy's name after leading his team to two victories in a row during the first two Super Bowls. However, how did this occur?

Vince Lombardi, who lost his fight with cancer in late 1970 at the age of 57, is remembered by the football trophy bearing his name. The trophy, which was formerly known as the "World Professional Football Championship Trophy," was renamed after the head coach and presented to the Baltimore Colts during Super Bowl V's matchup with the Dallas Cowboys the following year.

Records

In the NFL, you don't get points for winning or drawing games. Basically, a win counts for a win and a loss counts for a loss, and that also goes for a tie, which has been quite rare in recent times. What is obtainable is a win and a loss record. So, for instance, the team that comes out on top in the NFC East will potentially win ten games and lose six. However, in a division where two teams have the same records (same wins and losses), these are the possible tie breakers:

- ✓ Head-to-head (best won-lost-tied percentage in games between the clubs)
- ✓ Best won-lost-tied percentage in games played within the division
- ✓ Best won-lost-tied percentage in common games
- ✓ Best won-lost-tied percentage in games played within the conference
- ✓ Strength of victory in all games
- ✓ Strength of schedule in all games
- ✓ Best combined ranking among conference teams in points scored and points allowed in all games
- ✓ Best overall record for points scored and points conceded throughout all games among all teams

- ✓ Best net points in regular-season games
- ✓ Best net points across all contests

Free Agency

When a player's contract with a team expires in professional sports, they become free agents and are available to sign with any club or franchise. As the month of March comes around, so does NFL free agency. The current structure has been introduced since 1993, and the two main free agent categories are: restricted free agents and unrestricted free agents. Unrestricted free agent means that a player has completed four or more NFL seasons of service, whose contract has expired, and is free to sign with any team.

In the NFL, players with three or more seasons of service who have had their contracts expire are considered restricted free agents (RFAs). When their contracts expire, RFAs receive qualifying offers from their previous clubs. At this point, they are free to negotiate with any NFL club until a specific deadline, which usually falls approximately a week prior to the NFL Draft.

During this negotiation period, if a player receives an offer from a new club and chooses to accept it, the player's original club retains the right to match the offer and keep the player on their roster. However, if the original club decides not to match the offer made by the new club, they may receive draft-choice compensation based on the level of the qualifying offer extended to the player.

NFL Draft

Teams have the chance to bolster their rosters with fresh talent at the annual NFL Draft. Some players will instantly improve the squad that chooses them, while others won't. However, the possibility that recruited players can propel their new teams to glory drives teams to battle for talent, whether in the first or last round.

As the NFL has expanded and gained more fans, the draft has altered. The NFL regularly changes the draft and introduces new rules and regulations to preserve fairness in light of the competition for top players that exists both inside the league's clubs as well as outside between the NFL and upstart leagues.

The NFL draft comes in the months of April, where all 32 teams get one selection program up to seven total rounds to choose a collegiate that has declared for the draft or a player three years removed from high school. Each pick is timed, and the draft itself is nationally-televised.

2018 NFL DRAFT ORDER RD 1

#	Team	#	Team
1	BROWNS	17	CHARGERS
2	GIANTS	18	SEAHAWKS
3	COLTS	19	COWBOYS
4	TEXANS	20	LIONS
5	BRONCOS	21	
6	JETS	22	
7	BUCS	23	
8	BEARS	24	
9	49ERS	25	
10	RAIDERS	26	
11	DOLPHINS	27	
12	BENGALS	28	
13	REDSKINS	29	
14	PACKERS	30	
15	CARDINALS	31	
16	RAVENS	32	

The order of selection is chosen by the reverse order of finishes from the previous season. Without club trades, each round starts with the group that finished the regular season with the worst record and ends with the Super Bowl champions.

Picks 1-20 are for non-playoff teams based on their regular-season record, going from worst to best. Spot 21-24 are the teams that lost in the Wild-Card round, ranked on their regular-season report from worst to best. 25-28 are the divisional playoff teams who lost, and spots 29-30 are the conference championship teams who lost. The defeated club in the Super Bowl has the 31st choice in the draft. And finally, the Super Bowl champs pick last – 32.

With the order laid out, teams will negotiate by trading future picks and players on the roster to move up to select a desired rookie in the present draft. Because of this, the order changes for future draft rounds.

In cases where two teams concluded the previous season with identical records, draft position is determined by strength of schedule—the combined winning percentage of a team's opponents. The team with the lowest winning percentage during the schedule will be given the higher pick.

When teams play identically difficult opponents, divisional or conference tiebreakers are used to determine the winner. The following tie-breaking method will be employed if ties still exist between teams from different conferences or if the divisional or conference tiebreakers are not applicable:

- Head-to-head, if applicable
- Best win-loss-tie ratio in regular games (minimum four)
- Strength of win in all contests
- Best overall record for points scored and points conceded across all teams
- Best net points across all games
- Best net touchdowns across all contests
- Coin toss

Revenue

The NFL has three primary sources of revenue: NFL Venture, which handles the merchandising like jerseys and apparel; NFL Enterprises, which consists of the NFL Network and NFL Sunday ticket broadcasts; and Television Contracts, which is the bread and butter of the league, making up almost two-thirds of their entire revenue. TV is the reason why the salary cap has risen so much since 1994. With TV ratings increasing 5% from 2017 to 2018, NBC, CBS, EBS, and Fox, all race to see who can outbid each other whenever a new deal is negotiated. The numbers speak for themselves. In 2018, NFL games averaged 15.8 million viewers, excluding the London broadcasts. For the prime time games, the NFL has three nights of just one game being broadcast nationally: Thursday Night Football, Sunday Night Football, and Monday Night Football. Each of those nights had an increase in viewership from 2017.

As the Super Bowl crowns a champion and the season comes to a close, the league distributes its revenue equally among the 32 teams, regardless of performance, to make it fair.

CHAPTER SIX
TACTICS, STRATEGY AND SKILLS

American football places a lot of emphasis on strategy. Both teams prepare for play (attack) and defense (reaction) by planning several aspects of play, including the formation to use, who to field in, and the duties and instructions provided to each player. In order to win the game, each team adjusts to their opponent's noticeable strengths and weaknesses throughout the game and tries various strategies to outwit or overwhelm them. A team's offensive responsibility on the field is to score touchdown and field goals while keeping an eye on the opponent's defensive plan. On the defensive side of the ball, a team's job is to keep the offense from scoring touchdowns and field goals while also intercepting the ball.

Offensive Football Strategy

Offensive techniques are developed during football training and implemented throughout games. Numerous offensive tactics center on players taking various routes in the hopes of receiving a ball from the quarterback. Wide receivers and tight ends frequently employ strategies that entail catching deep passes. Some positions, such as offensive linemen, concentrate on thwarting defenders' attempts to sack the quarterback.

Running plays are part of other offensive strategies. These are sometimes employed when short-yardage gains are more essential than passes, specifically when a first down is close. Runs can also be utilized strategically to extend the clock's duration without running into the danger of a turnover. The offensive strategy a coach employs in a specific situation varies depending on variables including the score, amount of time left in the game, distance to cover, and the set-up of the opposition defense.

The spread offense is one well-known tactic. By dispersing the players over the field, this approach makes it more difficult for the defense to cover every player. Additionally, it increases the possibilities for rapid runs and short passes.

The play-action passing tactic is another potent offensive tactic. This strategy involves pretending to run a play before launching the ball downfield, which can surprise defenders and lead to significant gains.

Flea flickers and double-reverses are two trick moves that teams may use to fool their opponents and gain the upper hand on the offensive side.

Strong coach-player communication is essential for developing effective attacking schemes, as is meticulous analysis of the defenses and vulnerabilities of the opposition. Teams can overwhelm their opponents if these methods are implemented correctly.

Offense Basics

In football, the offense is the team with the ball. In order to keep possession of the ball, they have four downs to advance ten yards and secure a first down. The offense has two options for moving the ball: running and passing. Eleven players are on the field for each offensive play, the same number as on defense. On different plays, the precise positions will change.

Play begins with each team forming up on the line of scrimmage. On the line of scrimmage, there must be a minimum of seven players. When the ball is snapped, all players except one must be in position. There's a chance that one of the backfield players is "in motion" when the snap occurs. Each offensive play starts with the quarterback receiving the ball from the center.

Blocking - Blocking is a crucial component of any offensive play. Here, offensive players block the path of defensive players to stop them from tackling the ball-carrier. This is a challenging task since blockers are not to cling onto defensive players; NFL blocking strategies are complex. On every play, the players are given distinct tasks. The middle linebacker on the left may be blocked by the full back. The left defensive end could be pulled and blocked to the right by the right guard. On TV, everything appears chaotic, yet each participant is responsible for their own part. On running plays, blocking duties fall to the receivers as well. A successful block by a receiver on a cornerback can determine whether or not a team scores a touchdown.

Running Plays - The quarterback can either carry the ball himself during running plays or pass it to a running back. In exceptional cases, a receiver may race through the backfield to catch the ball on a running play.

- *Up the middle* - Running plays might be made to pass through a gap the defensive line has left. The running back in this scenario will attempt to scurry through the opening as soon as it appears. In order to keep the linebacker out of the way, he will occasionally follow the fullback through the hole where the fullback is.
- *Sweep* - The sweep rushing play aims to go beyond the defensive line's outside edge.
- *Draw* - In a draw running play, the quarterback retreats like he's trying to pass the ball before handing it to a running back, performing a decoy.

Passing Plays – A passing play involves the quarterback stepping back and delivering the ball to a suitable receiver. Usually, there is a main receiver on a play, but the quarterback will opt for other receivers if that one is covered. Wide receivers, slot receivers, tight ends, and running backs are among the players who catch the ball.

Here are a few instances of passing plays:

- *Down the field*: Longer throws down the field where the receiver runs quick routes like the fly and post. The offensive line must give the quarterback additional time to create this play.

- *Short pass*: Short passes do not gain as many initial yards as long passes, but they are extremely useful when the defense blitzes or the offensive line is having difficulty blocking. The curl, slant, and out are examples of common short pass routes.
- *Fade*: The fade route is frequently used when the offense gets near the goal line. The quarterback will throw the ball high into the air while a huge, tall receiver runs to the corner of the end zone. The towering receiver is expected to out-jump the cornerback to get the ball.
- *Screen pass*: A short pass into the backfield is referred to as a screen pass. Normally, offensive linemen will allow defensive linemen to pass them. The quarterback will then lob the ball to a running back just inches beyond the defensive linemen. The offensive lineman can now advance down the field and defend the running back from the linebackers.

Play Action - The quarterback fakes a handoff for a run before passing the ball in a maneuver known as *Play Action*. This is incredibly effective if the team has previously had success running. The linebackers and safeties will "bite" on the run and move in the direction of the line of scrimmage as a result of the fake handoff. The receivers may have an edge in finding openings for the throw as a result.

Offensive Formations

Watching an NFL football game can make you aware of how the offensive players line up somewhat differently for various plays. These various lineups are known as formations.

Each formation must adhere to the regulations (for instance, the line of scrimmage must have seven players present). Different formations are used for different play types. Below are some examples of offensive formations.

Single Back: The single back formation, often known as the ace formation, features one rushing back in the backfield with the quarterback behind center. This permit either three wide receivers and a tight end or four wide receivers. This formation allows teams to pass or run effectively.

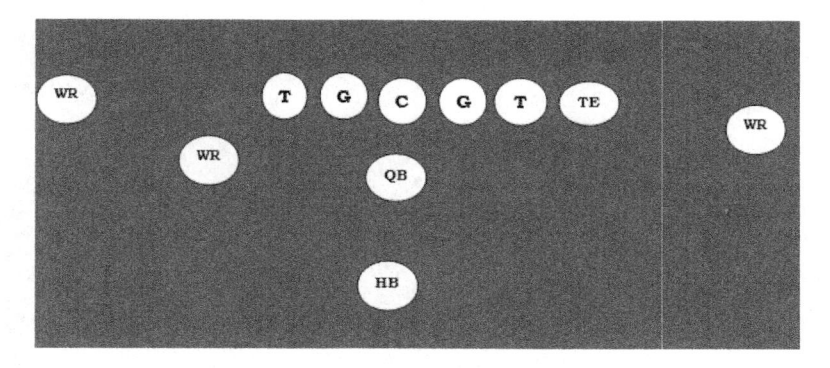

Pro Set: The pro set has two running backs, a fullback and a tailback. They are dispersed, with each person standing behind and to one side of the quarterback. The play is initiated by the quarterback under center.

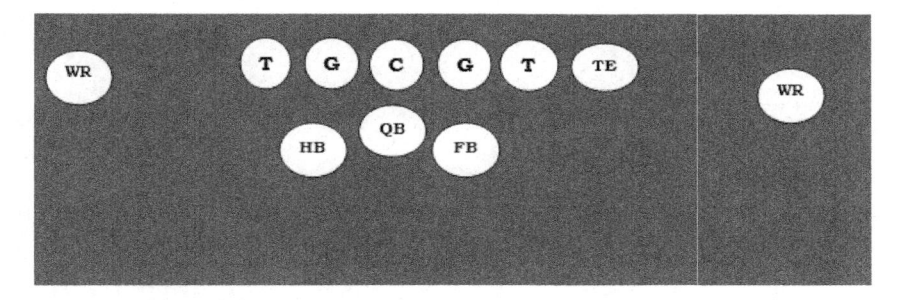

Empty Backfield: This formation sees the quarterback positioned under the center with no running backs—a true passing formation—allowing the team to field five wide receivers.

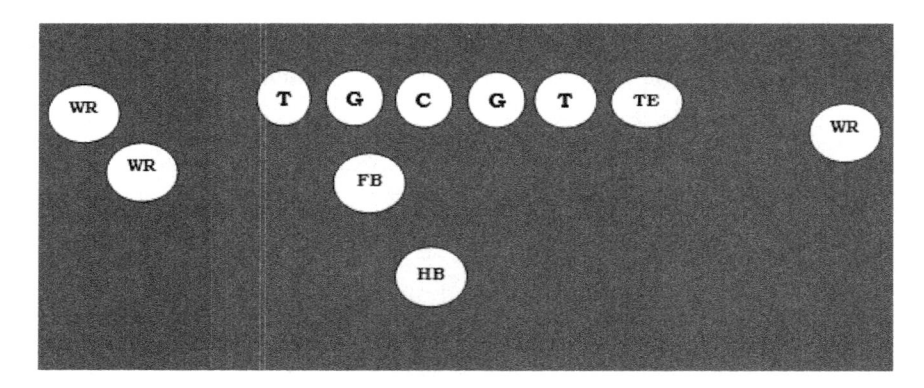

Spread Offense: The spread offense is intended to distribute the defense and open up the field for skilled and quick runners to work in. The shotgun formation is often used to run the spread offense, which usually has a lot of wide receivers.

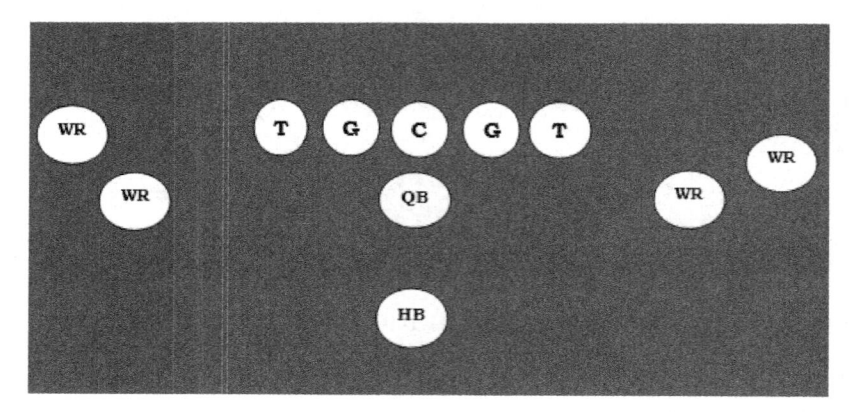

Wishbone: This is a running formation, featuring a fullback, two halfbacks, and three running backs. There can also be two tight ends and no wide receivers. This can signal to the opposition that you are running with the ball, but it also makes room for numerous blockers.

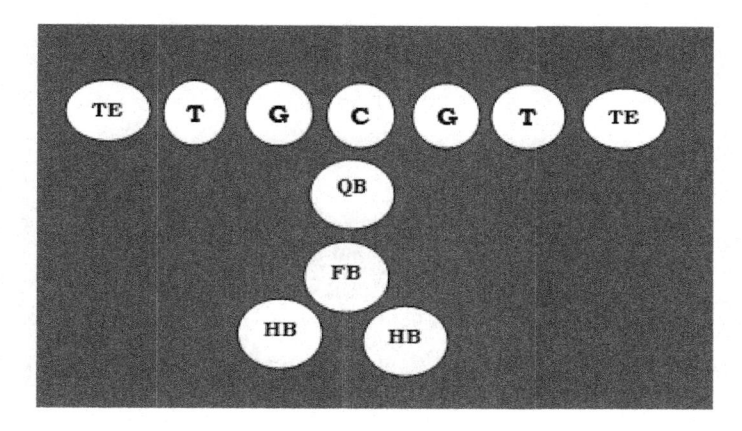

I Formation: The I formation sees two running backs lined up, with the quarterback under the center. Following the quarterback in a straight line, the fullback lines up, followed by the tailback. The fullback will typically rush through the hole first during a play, blocking any linebackers. The tailback will follow through with the ball after the fullback passes through the hole.

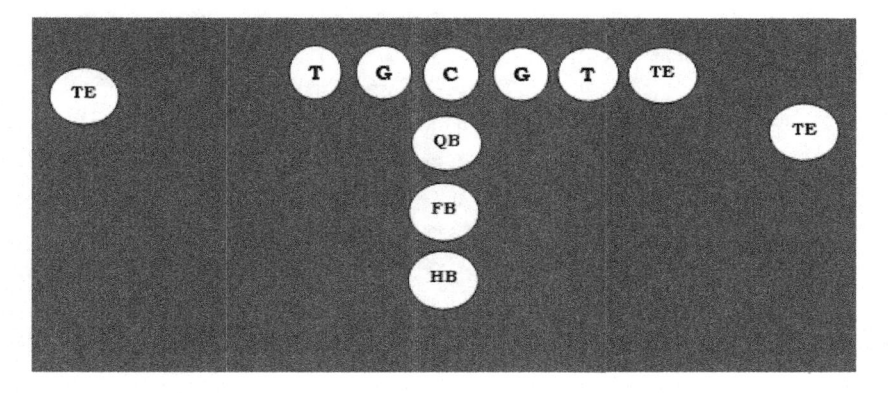

Goal Line Offense: This formation is one with ultimate power running designed to gain a few last yards necessary for a touchdown.

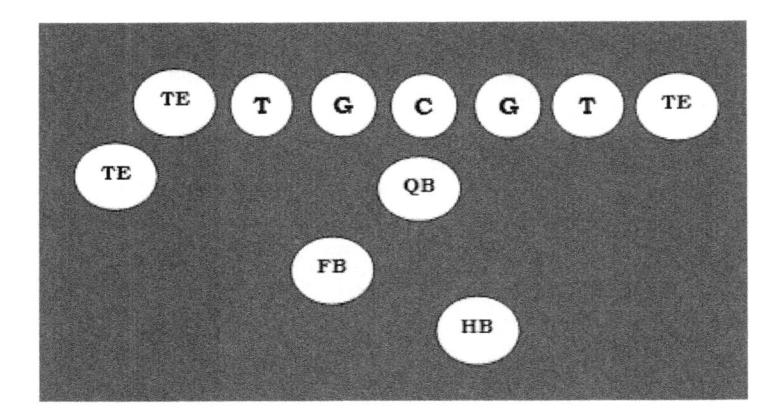

Shotgun Formation: The quarterback is positioned several feet behind the center in the shotgun formation. The center throws the ball to the quarterback in the air. This formation has the benefit of improving the quarterback's vision of the field and defenders. The drawback is that there are fewer running possibilities. The defense is aware that the play will probably end with a pass.

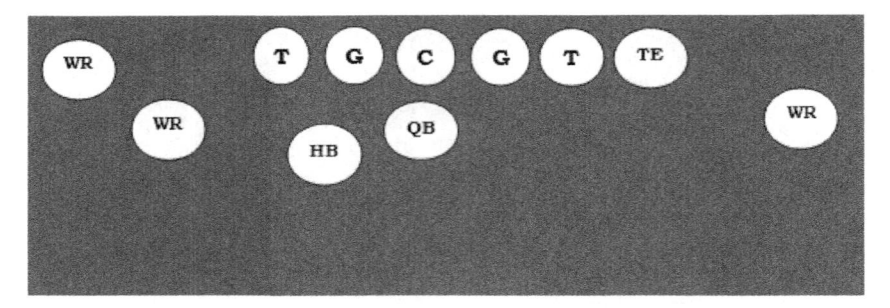

Wildcat: The Miami Dolphins made the wildcat formation gain popularity a few years ago. In this setup, the running back is positioned at quarterback area and carries the ball. Although the majority of the plays in this formation are running plays, an additional blocker for the runner is present because the quarterback is not in the backfield.

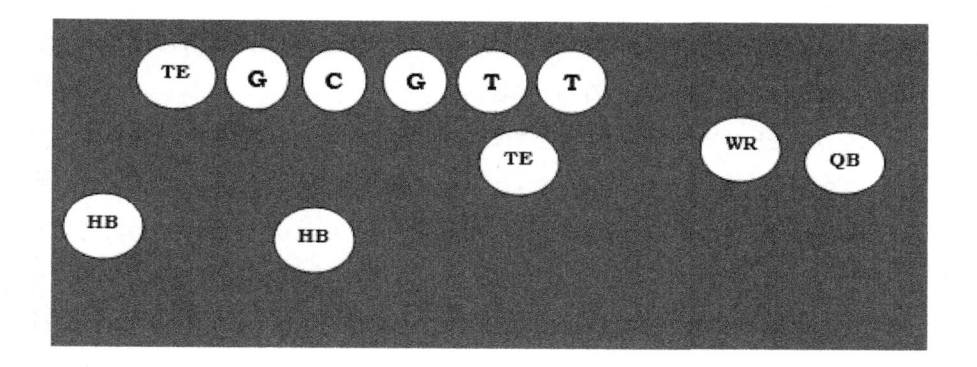

Passing Routes

The offense has the advantage over the defense because the quarterback anticipates the receiver's route since he understands it. In this manner, the quarterback can deliver the pass before the receiver arrives at the target. In order to succeed in the throwing game, practice and timing between the receiver and the quarterback are crucial.

What is a passing route?
Every play necessitates that the receiver follows a particular pattern or route. The route specifies both the receiver's intended direction and the total distance. The receiver might, for instance, run ten yards up the field before turning to face the sidelines.

The following is a list of common football pass routes:

1. **Flat** – This goes up and out to the side line.
2. **Slant** – When running a slant route, the receiver first travels a short distance down the field before making a rapid 45-degree cut across the middle of the field. This

is a nice route to use when facing blitz opponents or when making a short pass.
3. **Comeback** – A route that runs up the field, then cuts, coming back towards the quarterback.
4. **Curl** – Same as the comeback, but you turn towards the sideline.
5. **Out** – This is similar to the flat, but further up the field.
6. **In or Dig** – The In route, also known as the Dig route, is similar to the Out route except that the receiver makes a 90-degree cut to the center of the field.
7. **Corner** – Similar to the post route, the corner or flag route is typically used on longer plays. In the flag route, the receiver advances 10 to 15 yards up the field before turning and heading for the pylon in the end zone corner.
8. **Post** – This is another deep route, but your cut will be towards the field goal post, hence the name.
9. **Fly** – The receiver takes a direct path up the field on a fly route, using their speed to get past the CB. Sometimes they'll make an early move to appear to be running away or to fool the defender. Then they accelerate suddenly and run a fly route.

Route Trees – Route trees display every possible route that a receiver can take in one picture. The receiver can tell which route is a "1" and which is a "9" because they are usually numbered. This quickens and simplifies play-calling.

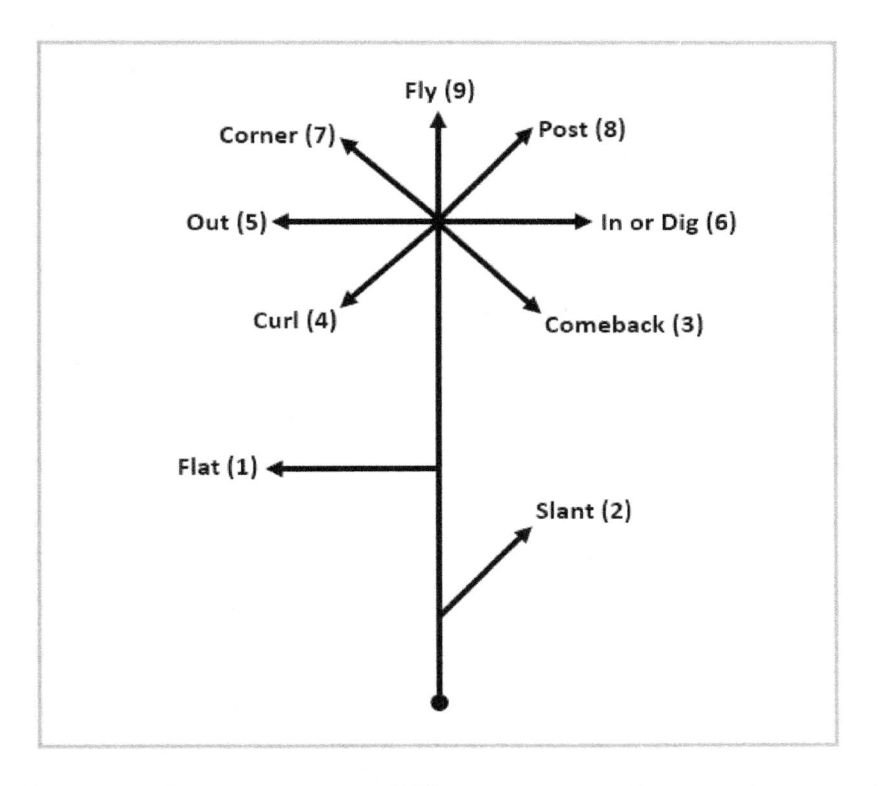

```
              Fly (9)
                ↑
   Corner (7) ↖ | ↗ Post (8)
                |
   Out (5) ←————+————→ In or Dig (6)
                |
   Curl (4) ↙   |   ↘ Comeback (3)
                |
                |
   Flat (1) ←———+
                |
                |    ↗ Slant (2)
                |   /
                |  /
                | /
                •
```

Option Reads: Numerous NFL teams employ option reads. Based on the defense, the receiver may choose to take a different route at this point. For example, if they want to run an "in" route but observe that the opposition is set up to defend the "in," they may decide to run an "out." This obviously requires study and practice. To avoid throwing an interception, the quarterback must be aware that the receiver is switching to the option route.

Defensive Football Strategy

In American football, defensive tactics are crucial. The primary goal of the defense is to prevent the opposing side from gaining points by tackling and intercepting passes. Teams employ a variety of defensive tactics based on their opponent's down, distance, field position, and time remaining.

Throughout a game, the defense utilizes the most different plays. They can therefore choose from a variety of strategies and formations based on how the other team initiates each play. The blitz, where five or more defenders pressure the quarterback in an effort to sack him, is one of the most popular defensive strategies. Another common tactic is the "prevent defense," which involves adding an extra defensive back to the defense and forcing the offense to make short passes rather than lengthy ones. Due to the fluid changes in position an offensive team can make, it is important for the defense to have a good knowledge of the best formation to counter them. Professional teams memorize dozens of plays.

The 3-4 system, which has four linebackers and three defensive linemen, is a popular defensive tactic. This formation keeps a powerful front against the run while allowing for additional flexibility in coverage and blitzing options.

Man-to-man coverage is another excellent defensive system in which each defender has a specific attacking player to cover throughout the game. Although it is challenging, it also offers close coverage, which makes it tough for quarterbacks to complete throws.

Zone defenses are also prevalent, in which defenders split the field into zones that they are responsible for covering. While this style of defense can help stop short or intermediate throws, it might also offer openings for longer throws.

Situational defenses, such as goal-line stands, force teams to concentrate on preventing their opponents from scoring when they have few yards remaining before reaching the end zone.

American football defensive strategies are critical in every game because they hold opposition offenses at bay while providing their own offensive opportunities to score and win games.

Defense Basics

When the opposing team has the ball, it is the defense's responsibility to stop them. The defense's goal is to keep the offense from gaining 10 yards in four plays. If they succeed, their team will regain possession of the ball, and their offense will come on. Defenses will also attempt to gain possession of the ball through a turnover, such as a fumble or interception.

Defensive Players – The defensive players are classified into three groups:
- *Defensive Line*: The defensive line consists of the big players on the line of scrimmage, such as the defensive tackles, nosetackles, and defensive ends. They stop the run and generate a pass rush.
- *Linebackers*: Linebackers are the primary tacklers on defense. These players line up just behind the defensive

line. They blitz, halt the run, and play pass defense against running backs and tight ends.
- *Secondary*: The secondary is the final line of defense, consisting of safeties and cornerbacks. Their primary responsibility is pass-defense; however, they also assist if runners get by the linebackers.

Tackling - The primary ability that all defensive players need to possess is tackling. If you can't tackle, it doesn't matter how quick you are, how effectively you can shed blockers, or how well-prepared you are; you won't be a competent defensive player.

Pre-Snap - The defense lines up before the snap. The middle linebacker typically makes the play calls. In the NFL, teams use a variety of defensive formations and strategies throughout the course of a game. When passing, they might have more players in the secondary, and when sprinting, they might have more players "in the box" up front.

Unlike the attack, the defense does not need to maintain its position. Before the snap, they are free to move as they choose. Defenses take advantage of this by shifting linemen around or faking to blitz before backing off in an effort to throw the quarterback off guard.

Key Off the Tight End - The tight end is frequently the focal point of the defensive alignment. Depending on which side the tight end lines up on, the middle linebacker will shout "left" or "right" in response. The defense will then adjust in line with that.

Run Defense - Any defense's primary objective is to halt the run. To do this, everyone involved cooperates. While they are catching the runner, the defensive lineman attempts to take on blockers. They make an effort to stop the runner from leaving the perimeter. Linebackers step up at the same moment to cover any gaps. The linebackers tackle the running back when he tries to slip through. The quick secondary players must track down the runner if he manages to evade the linemen and linebackers and stop a long run or touchdown.

Pass Defense - Passing has become a crucial component of most offenses; hence, pass defense is growing in importance. Once more, a strong pass defense requires cooperation from every member of the defense. While the linemen rush the quarterback, the linebackers and secondary cover the receivers. The less time the receivers have to find openings, the faster the lineman can rush the quarterback. However, the longer it takes the lineman to get to the quarterback, the better the secondary should do at containing the receivers.

Defensive Formations

Prior to each play, the defensive team will line up in a precise formation When the play starts, each player takes up a specific position on the field and is responsible for a specific task. Based on the play and circumstances, formations and roles will change throughout the course of the game. However, most teams employ a primary "base defense" that serves as the foundation for all other formations.

Base defenses are frequently named after the first two defensive lines. This refers to the linemen and linebackers. In a 4-3 defense, for instance, there are 4 linemen and 3 linebackers, whereas in a 3-4 defensive, there are 3 linemen and 4 linebackers. The 46 defense is distinctive in that it took its name from a safety by the name of Doug Plank, who participated in the initial iteration of the 46 defense and wore the jersey number 46.

The following are some of the most common base defense formations used in football today:

4-3 Defense: In the NFL, the 4-3 defensive formation is quite common. It uses two cornerbacks, two safeties, three linebackers, and four defensive linemen. In passing situations, more cornerbacks may take the place of the linebackers.

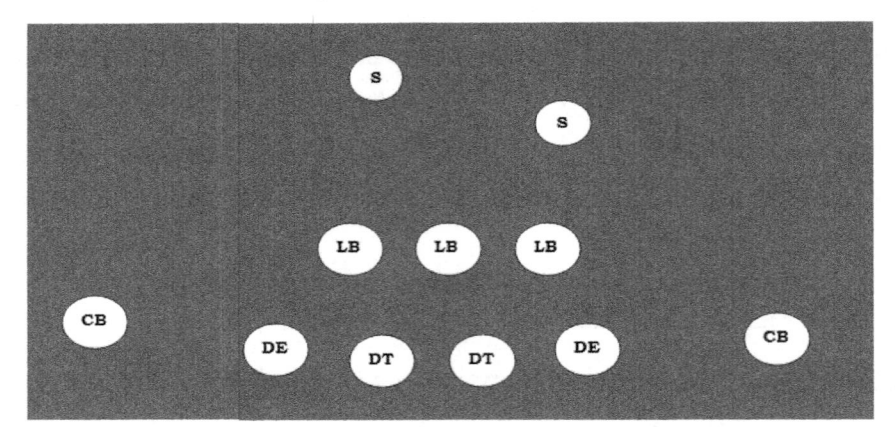

In the 4-3, the defensive ends are frequently the stars because they offer the outside pass rush and produce the most sacks. Because the defensive line is so important to this popular defense, defensive linemen are frequently selected as top picks and highly sought-after players.

3-4 Defense: Similar to the 4-3 system, the 3-4 defense substitutes a linebacker for a defensive lineman. The 3-4 defense has four linebackers, three linemen, two safeties, and two cornerbacks.

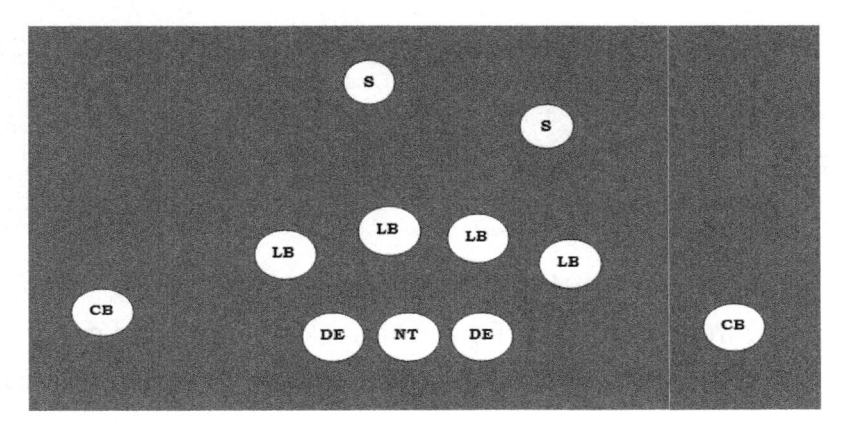

The 3-4 defense places emphasis on speed. Linebackers are tasked with covering the run as well as rushing the passer. The nose tackle needs to be a big man who can handle a few offensive linemen. The outside linebackers need to be strong and quick.

5-2 Defense: The 5-2 is designed to thwart the running attack. It has two linebackers and five defensive linemen. This is a prevalent defense in middle school and high school, where running is frequently the dominant offensive play.

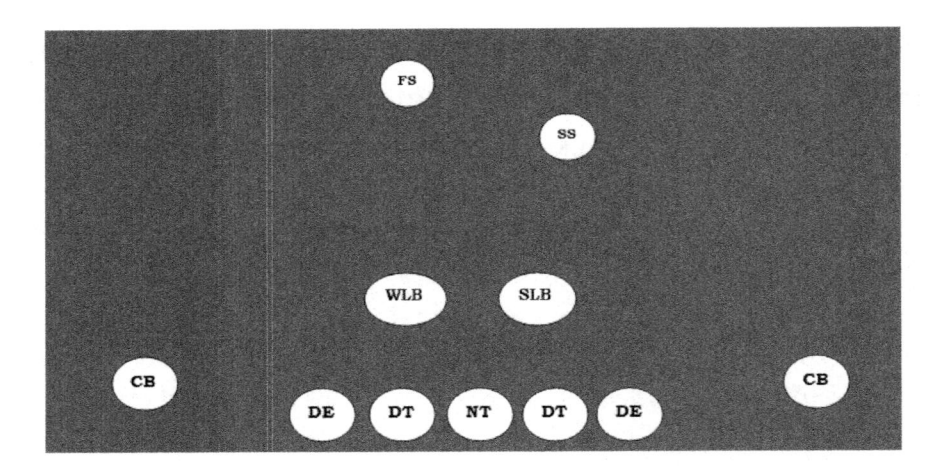

4-4 Defense: Another prominent defense to halt the running game is the 4-4. Four linebackers and four defensive linemen make up this defense. This makes it possible to have eight men in the box, which is excellent for stopping the run but leaves you open to a passing attack.

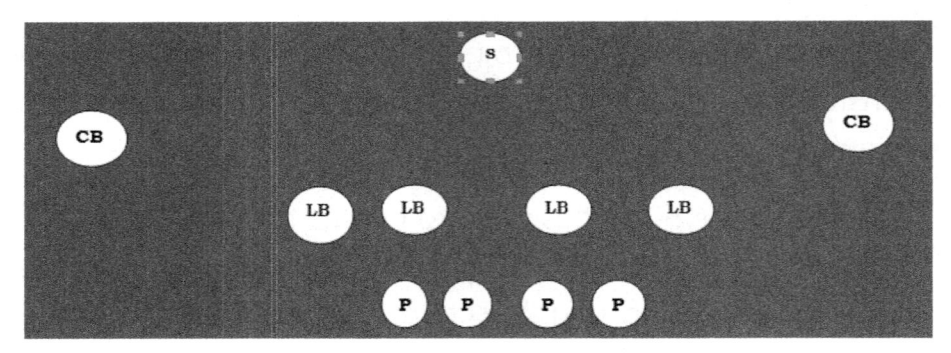

46 Defense: When playing the 46 defense, which is related to the 4-3 defensive, the strong safety can move up and play more like a linebacker. This formation provides a lot of versatility for the defense, but it requires a big, skilled, and strong safety.

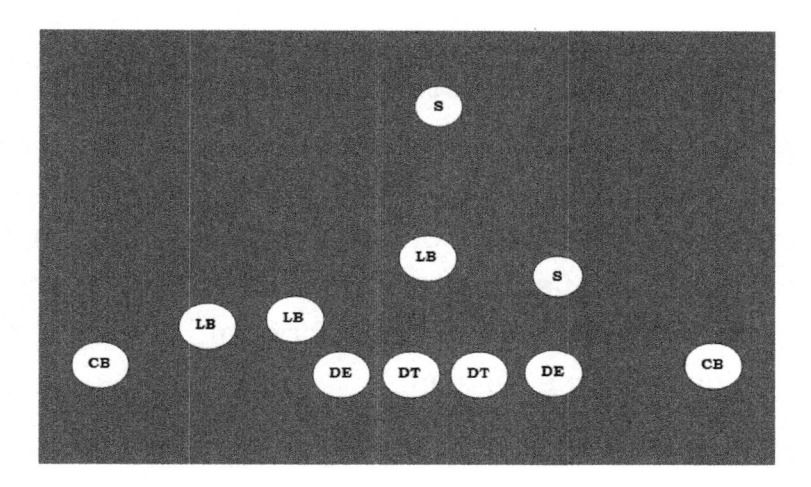

Nickel and Dime: Passing situations call for the nickel and dime defense. In the nickel, a fifth defensive back replaces a linebacker on the field. In the dime, a sixth defensive back replaces a linebacker.

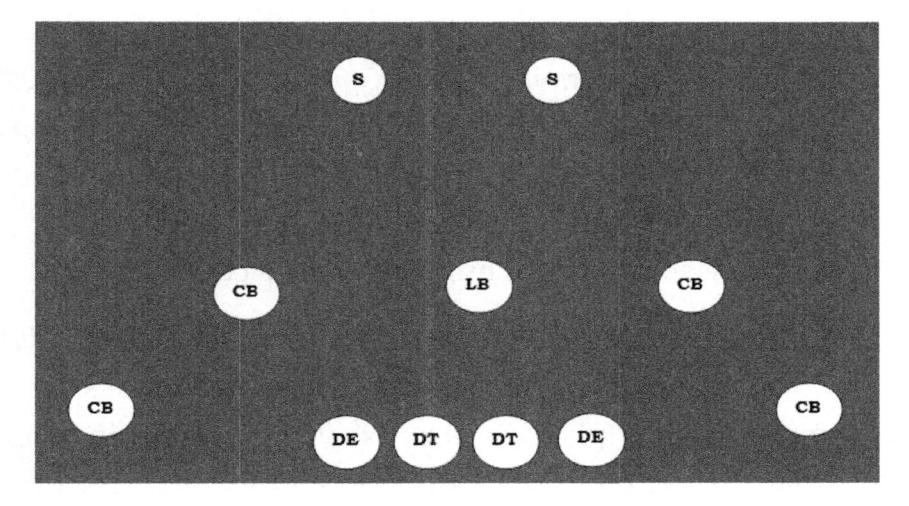

Prevent: On defense, a "prevent" play occurs when every defensive back drops deep to prevent a touchdown. When the offensive is facing a do-or-die situation, this play is typically used against a Hail Mary.

Special Team Strategies

Special teams indeed play a pivotal role in American football, often influencing the outcome of games. These units are responsible for handling various aspects of the game, such as kickoffs, punts, and field goals, and their strategies are critical for success. Here are some important strategies and considerations for special teams:

1. **Designated Returners**: Having designated returners for both kickoff and punt returns is essential. These players should possess attributes such as speed, agility, and the ability to catch the ball under pressure. They are responsible for fielding kicks and attempting to gain favorable field position for the offense.

2. **Blocking and Running Lanes**: Special team's units must focus on blocking for the returner and creating running lanes. Effective blocking can help the returner evade tackles and gain additional yardage. Well-executed blocking schemes are essential for successful returns.

3. **Coverage**: Equally important is having effective coverage on kickoffs and punts. Special team's units must include players who excel at tackling in open space. This helps prevent the opposing team's returner from making significant gains and provides better field position for the defense.

4. **Fake Kicks**: Special teams can employ fake kicks as a surprise tactic, but these plays require precise

execution and perfect timing. A failed fake kick attempt can result in a turnover, so they should be used judiciously and with careful planning.

5. **Adaptation to Weather**: Special teams coaches need to adjust their strategies based on weather conditions. Adverse weather, such as strong winds or heavy rain, can affect kicking distance and accuracy. Coaches may need to modify their approach to account for these conditions, including making adjustments to kick trajectories and distances.

6. **Field Position**: Special team plays can significantly impact field position, which can, in turn, affect the overall flow of the game. Teams that consistently win the field position battle often have an advantage in terms of scoring opportunities and defensive positioning.

Overall, special teams represent a critical phase of the game that demands careful planning, execution, and attention to detail. Successful special teams play can provide a team with field position advantages, create scoring opportunities, and even swing the momentum of a game in their favor.

Game Management Strategies

Game management strategies in American football encompass the various tactics and decisions that coaches employ during a game to increase their team's chances of securing a victory. These strategies are essential for optimizing a team's performance and outcome. Here are some key aspects of game management in football:

1. **Clock Management**: Teams aim to control the amount of time left on the game clock, especially in critical situations. Strategies include running or passing plays that can either run down the clock or stop it when necessary. This becomes particularly important in late-game scenarios when preserving a lead or attempting a comeback.

2. **Situational Play-Calling**: Coaches make play-calling decisions based on the specific situation in the game. This includes considering factors like field position, Down and yardage, time remaining, and the score. For instance, in short-yardage situations near their end zone, teams may opt for low-risk plays to avoid turnovers.

3. **Player Management**: Coaches must monitor player fatigue and injuries throughout the game. This involves rotating players when needed to keep them fresh and ensuring they stay hydrated and rested during breaks. Managing the physical condition of players is crucial for sustaining peak performance.

4. **Effective Use of Timeouts**: Coaches use timeouts strategically to stop the game clock, regroup their team, discuss plays, or challenge referee decisions. The timing and purpose of timeouts can significantly impact the flow and outcome of a game.

5. **Challenges and Instant Replay**: Coaches can challenge on-field rulings through instant replay review. This resource allows them to contest specific calls and potentially reverse unfavorable decisions, affecting the course of the game.

Effective game management involves a combination of tactical decision-making, situational awareness, and resource utilization. Coaches aim to exploit their team's strengths while countering the opponent's strategies to secure a favorable outcome. By carefully executing these game management strategies, teams can gain a competitive edge and increase their chances of success on the football field.

Football Skills

Football is a challenging sport that calls on a wide range of skills. Each player possesses specific skills related to their field position. For instance, one player can be tasked with catching passes, while another might be tasked with kicking the ball. There are 11 players on the field for each team, each doing a specific task. The most essential skills for playing any position in football are described in the following paragraphs.

Offensive Skills

Blocking: Blocking is sometimes the most underappreciated component of football, although it is critical to the offense's success. To block, an offensive player steps in front of a defender and prevents them from rushing the quarterback or tackling a player with the ball.

When run blocking, the blockers' job is to make openings in the defense that the ball carrier can use to get through. In pass blocking, offensive linemen and occasionally running backs drop back to keep the quarterback safe from the opposition's hits.

Although running backs, tight ends, and receivers also block, offensive linemen have it as their primary task. It will be difficult for the offense to be successful in pushing the ball down the field without strong blocking.

Catching: Tight ends, wide receivers, and occasionally running backs are responsible for catching passes from the quarterback. Having good pass-catchers is almost as vital as having a competent quarterback. Wide receivers, who excel at securing the football in the air, handle the majority of pass-catching. Running backs and tight ends are frequently used to catch dump-offs and shorter routes to get easy yards when they are not blocking during pass plays.

Passing: The ability to efficiently pass a football is essential for the success of any team. The quarterback is responsible for passing the ball, and he or she must possess certain abilities, such as strength and accuracy. The quarterback position is the most crucial position in football since passing is essential to having a successful offense. The quarterback must not only be physically capable of passing the ball well but also possess the mental capacity to judge where and when to throw the ball based on how the defense is positioned.

Reading the Defense: A good quarterback must be able to discern the plays that the defense calls and change their offensive plan accordingly. A good quarterback will be able to read the defense at the line of scrimmage and make audible calls based on the defense's play. For example, the offense might want to run the ball, but the quarterback realizes the defense is preparing to run a blitz. The quarterback switches the play at the line of scrimmage and tells his teammates they will pass the ball instead.

Route Running: Proper route running enables the quarterback to anticipate where to throw the ball while also allowing the runner to gain space from the defense. Route running is an essential skill for tight ends, wide receivers, and running backs.

Wide receivers typically run a variety of routes and should have a good balance of strength, speed, and size. Tight ends tend to run shallow routes more often, but they should be physically dominant and alert to detect defensive gaps. The majority of running back routes start in the backfield.

Running: When offenses don't pass the ball, they run it. Although all players on the pitch must run to some extent, running backs are especially necessary to have this skill. The running back's job is to carry the football and assist the offense in moving down the field. To avoid being tackled by defenders, running backs must have agility, speed, elusiveness, strength, and power.

Defensive Skills

Blitz: This is when the linemen, linebackers, and cornerbacks all rush the quarterback at once, while the safeties step a little in for the cornerbacks.

Tackling: Although different defensive positions necessitate different skills, every defensive player must be able to tackle. Tackling should be started by a good approach and footwork, along with an efficient contact of the shoulder to the thigh of the opponent, while wrapping the legs with your hands to immobilize the ball carrier and finishing well on top of the opponent.

Tackling is an important part of football because it prevents attacking players from moving the ball down the field. Defensive players must be able to tackle legally without incurring a penalty. Any tackle that involves hands on the offensive player's facemask or helmet-to-helmet contact is illegal.

Pass Defending: If the defense is unable to sack the quarterback and stop the ball from being launched, the next best thing is to prevent the ball from being caught by the receiver. Protecting passes that the quarterback throws is mostly the responsibility of cornerbacks and safeties. These defensive players must be quick enough to follow receivers and have good eye-to-hand coordination in order to track down the football that has been thrown and prevent it from being caught.

Pass Rushing: Since passing is an essential skill on the offensive side, the ability to rush the passer is crucial on the defense. Pass rushers need to be strong and agile in order to evade or overwhelm the offensive lineman and put pressure on the quarterback. The ability to disrupt an offense's passing game is critical to the defense's success. Pass rushers are mostly linebackers and defensive linemen, but safeties and cornerbacks can get involved.

Run Stopping: In addition to defending the pass, defensive players must also stop the run. Defensive linemen and linebackers must be strong, big, and fast enough to swarm the line of scrimmage while cutting off space for running backs. If the defense can neutralize the rushing game, the offense is forced to become one-dimensional by relying largely on the passing game. As a result, the defense has a better chance of success because they are primarily concerned with defending the pass at this stage.

Forcing Turnovers: A final crucial skill set for defensive players is the ability to force turnovers, such as interceptions, turnovers on downs, and fumbles, among others. Fumbles can be caused by defenders snatching the ball out of an offensive player's hands or tackling him so that he drops the ball before dropping to his knees.

To cause interceptions, defenders must be aware of the quarterback and attempt to forecast where he will throw the ball so that they can properly position themselves to collect the ball before the offensive receiver. And lastly, general turnovers on downs demand mastery in rushing, blocking, and tackling.

Special Team Skills

Kicking: Kicking is an exceptional skill that is typically only possessed by special team members. The place kicker's responsibility is to attempt to score points for their team by kicking the ball through the uprights of a field goal. Kickers need to have powerful legs and good precision to do this. Kickers must be able to advance the ball downfield on kickoffs in addition to making field goals and extra points. This demands a significant level of leg power.

Punting: Punters, like kickers, rely on their leg power and precision to do their jobs well. The punter's goal is to kick the ball as far as possible downfield without placing it in the end zone. A skilled punter puts his team's defense in a good field position.

Punt and Kick Returning: Fielding kicks and punts from the opposition's team gives returners the chance to earn yardage for their offense. Kick returners must be quick and elusive to avoid being tackled, just like receivers and running backs. Special teams are frequently an underrated aspect of the game, but having a strong kick returner may give teams a significant edge.

Covering Kickoffs and Punts: To prevent a touchdown or a lengthy return, players on the kicking team must race down the field and attempt to tackle the kick returner. The role needs both strength and quickness to outmuscle the returning team's blockers while closing in on the returner. Additionally, players must have the self-control to stay in their lanes and cover their assigned area of the field. Players that deviate from their lane can be exploited by kick returners, who can use these openings to gain more yards.

Techniques in Football

Swim Move

The swim move is a football tactic used by defensive linemen and linebackers to get around the blocking of the offensive line and rush the quarterback. The action is referred to as a swim since it mimics a swimmer's stroke. Players typically utilize the swim move when they are confronted by a blocker who is shorter or less powerful.

To perform a strong swim move, a player must have good coordination because they must move both their arms and feet at the same time. After the snap of the ball, the defensive player begins by taking quick and calculated jab steps. These steps are designed to confuse the blocker and momentarily freeze their movements. They will then reach out and push the offensive lineman's upper chest or shoulder while using the arm to their side with which they are swimming.

The push will knock the blocker off-balance, allowing the player to get through more easily. The other arm is then gently slipped over the defender's shoulder to complete the movement. Then, simultaneously with the arm movements, the player shifts their entire body to the side, away from the offensive lineman. This lateral movement further destabilizes the blocker and allows the defensive player to disengage completely.

Dip and Rip

Linebackers in football employ the dip and rip technique to slip past offensive line blocking and into a gap. By doing this, linebackers can breach the ball carrier's defense, allowing them to either sack the quarterback or halt a run. A good linebacker must be able to perform a dip and rip maneuver effectively and appropriately.

The goal of a dip and rip motion is to avoid an offensive lineman's block. Linebackers are frequently quicker and more agile than offensive linemen, which must be exploited when executing the move. When the play begins, the linebacker must move quickly and forcefully in the direction of the opening they are attempting to attack.

If the first step is executed well, the linemen will already be at a disadvantage and will thus rely on their strength to block a player, seeking to grasp and hold the linebacker. To counteract the block, the linebacker initiates the "dip" phase by lowering their shoulder and stepping with his outside foot to get clear into the gap that he is attacking. The lowering of the shoulder allows them to slip under the grasp of the blocker and avoid being held.

Following the dip, the linebacker executes the "rip" phase. This involves a forceful and upward motion with their arms, particularly the arm on the side opposite to the direction of the dip, and stepping their inside leg through to clear the blocker. The ripping motion is designed to break free from the blocker's grip. This leaves the blocker off-balance and struggling to regain control. The linebacker must then track down the ball carrier and attack them after getting rid of the block.

Blocking
The act of blocking involves an offensive player using their body to restrict a defender's path. Blocking is also used in special team plays in football. A blocker will do everything possible to obstruct a defender's path to the passer or ball carrier, based on the situation. Blockers accomplish this by making contact with the defensive player, blocking him from progressing towards the player with the ball, and therefore preventing a tackle.

Blocking demands proper technique. A blocker must first prepare their stance by placing their feet shoulder width apart, having their hands ready at their waist, and keeping their shoulders back and heads up. Then, immediately after the snap, they take an explosive first step at the defender, referred to as the "get off". The blocker will then make their strike by taking a second step and launching the block with their extended arms, contacting the opponent in the chest. They complete the block by lowering their waist, maintaining a broad base, and using their arms to dominate the defender.

Legal and Illegal Blocking

According to the NFL rulebook, blockers are allowed to utilize their whole body unless specifically prohibited. As a result, legal blocking may involve the use of the head, shoulders, hands, and outside of the forearms, in addition to other body parts.

However, there are a few limitations to blocking. The blocker's hands must go to the inside of the defensive player's body as soon as they start to block; however, the contact given to the defender must be below the neck and might be on the outside of the defensive player's body. This is done to avoid a material constraint, which usually entails grabbing a defensive player and manipulating them in some way—tackling, twisting, or forcing them to the ground, for example.

Blocking methods that result in a penalty include hand contact at or above the neck region, a block to the back, and material restrictions. Some of these regulations include exceptions, such as the generally prohibited practice of blocking in the back. Instances where blocking in the back is acceptable include recovering a loose ball, spinning to present one's back just before the block, and placing hands on the defending player's side.

Other prohibited blocking methods include clipping, illegal "peel back" blocks, chop blocks, low blocks, crackback blocks, and below-the-waist blocks on kicks and possession changes. However, in some circumstances, specific tactics are acceptable, such as the "peel back" block, which is acceptable when the blocker strikes the defensive player's frontside.

Although every offensive player blocks once in a while, some players block more frequently than others. The primary function of the offensive lineman is to provide blocking for the pass or run. The offensive line is made up of the right and left tackles, right and left guards, and center, all of whom are large enough to block for the whole time of the match. Although it is not their major duty, blocking can also be done by running backs, wide receivers, fullbacks, and tight ends to either assist the ball carrier or safeguard the quarterback.

Stances
Stances are the positions that defenders take before the snap is made.

2-Point Stance - The 2-point stance is a tactic utilized by numerous positions on the football field. Football players choose several stances in order to better position themselves for game situations. Their stance is also heavily influenced by the position they play. The number in the stance name is based on how many points on the player's body are in contact with the ground. In the 2-point stance, this indicates that only the player's two feet are in contact with the ground.

The 2-point stance is most widely used by running backs because it provides maximum field vision, easier adaptation, and better reaction time against defensive players. Players may, however, employ alternative stances and switch between them at any time during the game. For offensive players, the stance is particularly crucial because they must remain totally motionless prior to the ball being snapped in order to avoid a false start penalty. The 2-point stance is the most upright and allows players to adjust their motion more easily; it is also one of the most common football stances. The 2-point stance is also used by outside offensive linemen because it allows for swifter lateral movement and better response time to resisting defensive players.

A downside to the 2-point stance is that you do not begin with a low center of gravity, making it easier for your opponent to push you off balance. For instance, linemen can leap up into opposing players because their entire body is low to the ground when they line up in a 3- or 4-point stance. In contrast, it is easier to knock a lineman out of position if he is in a 2-point stance.

In a football game, using a 2-point stance requires proper technique. Players should stand with their feet shoulder-width apart on the ground. Based on where they are on the field and where the opposition team is positioned, some players stagger their feet for more stability. After establishing their stance and feet, players will face the line of scrimmage while looking up and surveying the field. With their knees slightly bent, the player should be balanced, with their weight evenly distributed. The hands are on the thighs but are poised to immediately rise in anticipation of blocking.

The most crucial thing a player must keep in mind is not to overly lean into their posture. To maintain balance, it's crucial to keep the back slightly curved while keeping the body upright.

3-Point Stance - The three-point stance is a football position used by offensive linemen, defensive linemen, and running backs in which, both of their feet and one hand have contact with the ground. Football players use several stances to position themselves more effectively for game scenarios; the stance they adopt is heavily influenced by the position they are playing.

In a football game, using a three-point stance requires proper form. Players should stand with their feet shoulder-width apart on the ground. Depending on where they are on the field and how the opposition team is positioned, some players will stagger their feet to provide balance and to get off to a faster start. Next, kneel while bending over and resting one hand's fingers on the ground for support.

To keep their balance and avoid being quickly knocked over by the defense, offensive linemen would put a little pressure on the hand that is on the ground. To launch themselves toward the offense at the snap of the ball, defensive linemen would lean slightly more into their stance. Face the line of scrimmage, elevate your head, and draw your shoulder blades back to broaden your chest.

The three-point stance is most frequently used by offensive and defensive linemen because it enables them to start quickly and explosively, acquire greater force from their legs, and stay low to move in any direction. The three-point stance is one of the most common stances for linemen; however, other stances can be used, and players can switch between different stances at any time over the course of the game. Since offensive players must remain totally motionless prior to the ball being snapped in order to avoid a false start penalty, this stance becomes an important one for them.

However, the three-point stance's position makes it considerably simpler for helmet contact to happen and for a penalty to be called. Thus, dropping into a three-point stance is riskier for linemen. In fact, because of the higher danger of head injuries it presents, the three-point stance is prohibited in major youth leagues like Pop Warner.

4-Point Stance - The player is in a four-point stance with both hands and both feet on the ground. The least used stance in football is the four-point stance. The four-point stance is occasionally used by offensive and defensive linemen to maximize their strength, leverage, and explosiveness in one direction. Even though linemen rarely use the four-point stance, it is one of the most effective positions for short-yardage or goal scenarios. The four-point stance does have some drawbacks, though, as players do not have as much room to maneuver laterally.

For offensive linemen, this stance can be particularly crucial in circumstances where they have to make a quick push forward. Similarly, it can be beneficial to defensive linemen in situations where they must cease being pushed back, stop an obvious running play, or get to a passer/ball carrier quickly.

In a football game, using a four-point stance requires proper technique. Most coaches will advise players to get down on their hands and knees with all of their toes touching the ground in order to take on the four-point stance position. Next, lift your hips and knees off the ground while shifting your weight to your feet and hands. In line with their position on the field and the positioning of the opposing team, some players will slightly stagger their feet to add balance and get off to a faster start.

To perform a perfect four-point stance, keep your knees bent and your back flat. Lean into your stance and distribute your weight evenly, keeping in mind that explosiveness is what the four-point stance is meant to foster. As you face the line of scrimmage, lift your head up to look at the field in front of you and draw your shoulder blades back to broaden up your chest.

Bull Rush

A bull rush is a football technique employed by pass rushers, including linemen and sometimes defensive ends, to defeat quarterback blocks. Unlike other pass-rushing strategies that rely more on fast hands and agile feet, the bull rush strategy is based on raw force.

A bull rush is when a defender makes hard first contact with an offensive lineman with both hands and attempts to force them backward. Following that, the defender will try to gain control, slip away from the lineman, and sack the quarterback.

The pass rusher must initially crouch lower than their opponent in order to gain advantage when using the bull rush technique. They must then extend their arms and try to keep themselves on the inside of the opponent's frame as they shoot their hands into the offensive lineman's chest. When employing this move, the defender should be positioned with their body forward, knees bent, and feet planted firmly on the ground. Their feet should also be moving continuously.

Bull rushes are the best way to demoralize the offense and demonstrate your defensive prowess. The bull rush works best when deployed by defensive lineman while other pass rushers encircle the pocket. Ideally, the quarterback won't be able to move because an offensive lineman will be pushed straight at them.

After pushing the blocker further back, the pass rusher can resort to another technique, such as the swim or rip move, to really get to the quarterback. At this time, the passer will likely be sacked or put under more pressure.

Key Plays

Draw Play – The play appears to be a pass play when it first begins. From center, the quarterback receives the snap before running back to make a throw. Instead of passing the ball, he hands it to a running back.

The reason it's called a draw is because it "draws" the opposing linemen in to go after the quarterback only to discover that he doesn't have the ball. The plan is to allow the running back to outrun the defenders who are closing in on the quarterback.

Play-Action Pass – This is contrary to a draw play. It should be termed a fake run since that is exactly what it is. The quarterback pretends to hand off the ball to a running back who is advancing toward the goal line as soon as the snap is taken. While the defenders try to tackle the player, they believe has the ball, the quarterback gets enough space in the field beyond the line of scrimmage to pass the ball.

Flea Flicker – This is a variation on the play-action pass. After receiving the snap, the quarterback passes the ball to the running back or tosses it to him. Then, the running back returns the ball back to the quarterback, who executes a pass play. This is a deceitful but dangerous play that often ends up in a turnover.

Quarterback Sneak: This play is tried when the first down line or the goal line are only a few yards away. After receiving the snap, the quarterback tries to lunge over the line. It's not an easy play since defensive linemen often anticipate a sneak play at such short distance.

About the Author

Edward Weber is a passionate sports enthusiast and an avid fan of American football, with a special love for the National Football League (NFL). With over a decade of experience following the NFL, Edward has become a dedicated aficionado of the game, from the nail-biting action on the field to the rich history and strategy that make American football such a captivating sport.

As a lifelong learner and teacher, Edward brings his expertise to this beginner's guide, aiming to demystify the NFL for newcomers to the sport. He understands the challenges faced by those just getting into football and believes that everyone should have the opportunity to enjoy the excitement and drama that the NFL has to offer.

Edward's writing is characterized by its accessibility and clarity, making complex concepts and rules easy to understand for readers of all levels of football knowledge. With this beginner's guide, he hopes to help you embark on your own NFL journey, whether it's for the love of the game, fantasy football, or simply to better understand the sport that captivates millions every year.

Edward Weber's beginner's guide to the NFL is the perfect starting point for anyone looking to dive into the exciting world of American football. With his insights, you'll gain the knowledge and confidence needed to appreciate and enjoy every touchdown, tackle, and triumph in the NFL.

Printed in Great Britain
by Amazon